How to Develop Your Child's Gifts and Talents in **Writing**

Other books by Martha Cheney

How to Develop Your Child's Gifts and Talents in Vocabulary
How to Develop Your Child's Gifts and Talents in Reading
Gifted & Talented® Reading, Book Two, 4–6
Gifted & Talented® Reading Puzzles & Games, 4–6
Gifted & Talented® Reading Comprehension, 6–8
Gifted & Talented® Puzzles & Games for Reading and Math,
    Book Two, 6–8
Gifted & Talented® Phonics, 4–6
Gifted & Talented® Phonics, 6–8
Gifted & Talented® Phonics Puzzles & Games, 4–6
Gifted & Talented® Phonics Puzzles & Games, 6–8
Gifted & Talented® Math, Book Two, 4–6
Gifted & Talented® Math Puzzles & Games, 4–6
Monster Math, Book Two
Monster Math Puzzles & Games, 6–8

with Diane Bockwoldt
Gifted & Talented® Puzzles & Games for Critical and Creative
    Thinking

with Mary Hill
Gifted & Talented® Atlas
Gifted & Talented® Almanac

with Evelyn Pesiri
Gifted & Talented® Dictionary
Gifted & Talented® Wordbook

with Mary Cron
Monster Math, Book One

How to Develop Your Child's Gifts and Talents in Writing

by Martha Cheney

LOWELL HOUSE

LOS ANGELES

CONTEMPORARY BOOKS

CHICAGO

Library of Congress Cataloging in Publication Data

Cheney, Martha.
    How to develop your child's gifts and talents in writing / by
    Martha Cheney.
        p.   cm.
    ISBN 1-56565-797-7
    1. English language—Composition and exercise—Study and teaching
    (Preschool)—United States. 2. English language—Composition and
exercise—Study and teaching (Elementary)—United States.
3. Education—Parent participation—United States. 4. Activity
programs in education—United States. 5. Creative activities and
seat work.   I. Title.
LB1140.5.L3C44   1997   97—34643
64′ .68—dc21   CIP

Requests for such permissions should be addressed to:
Lowell House
2020 Avenue of the Stars, Suite 300
Los Angeles, CA 90067

Lowell House books can be purchased at special discounts when ordered in
bulk for premiums and special sales.

Publisher: Jack Artenstein
Associate Publisher, Lowell House Adult: Bud Sperry
Managing Editor: Maria Magallanes
Text design: Brenda Leach / Once Upon a Design
Illustrations by Eve Guianan and Brenda Leach

Manufactured in the United States of America
10 9 8 7 6 5 4 3 2 1

For Gary, with love and gratitude

Note to Parents:

As you look through the suggested activities in this book, please keep in mind that they are designed and intended to be fun for you and your child. Choose only those that sound enjoyable. Don't try to do too much in one sitting. Follow your child's interest level. If an activity seems too difficult, put it aside and come back to it later. If an activity seems too easy, try to think of a way to make it more challenging, or go on to something else. Remember that the ultimate goal is to increase your child's desire to write and to help him or her discover the joy of self-expression.

It is important that your child have appropriate materials and a good place to work. A very young child needs only unlined paper in a variety of sizes and colors. Markers, crayons, paints, and chalk are fun for all ages. An older child needs lined paper (appropriate to his or her age), unlined paper, pens, and pencils, as well as an assortment of art materials. If possible, provide a desk from which the child can readily access all of these items and where he or she can comfortably work. If you don't have room for a desk, a cardboard storage box and the kitchen table will do just fine.

Also, remember that your participation is key to the success of these activities. They should not be used as "assignments." Most children have plenty of those within the context of school and homework. These investigations into the world of writing should be entered into together, in the spirit of exploration. Your investment of time and energy will help to spark your child's interest.

Contents

Introduction

The History of Writing

When we think of how writing began, most of us think of the alphabet. But writing got its start long before the invention of the alphabet. At some undetermined point in humankind's past, our prehistoric ancestors developed the capacity for speech. They began to relate objects and ideas to certain sound symbols. They began to communicate.

As communication, however, speech has necessary limitations. First, it is temporary. Speech is ephemeral, dying as quickly as it is born, enduring only in memory. Second, it is limited by space. Only those within the sound of the speaker's voice can receive the communication. As the sophistication of our ancestors increased, so did their desire for more effective communication. And somewhere in the neighborhood of 40,000 years ago, they began the journey toward more permanent and transportable communication—a journey that has been gathering speed ever since!

Pictures made on cave walls are among the earliest examples of the efforts of prehistoric man to communicate in a more lasting way. Exactly what these early "writers" wanted us to understand about the animal figures and symbols they scratched or painted onto the stone's surface we will never know, but we can certainly understand that they were important to our predecessors, and even that rudimentary communication, coming down to us over the millennia, is thrilling.

Prehistoric people made pictographs and petroglyphs on the walls of caves. Pictographs were created by drawing or painting, while petroglyphs were carved or scratched into the stone.

Eventually, a more complex system of picture writing evolved. Pictures were grouped together to tell a story or communicate an idea. These groupings of pictures are referred to as ideograms. Similar ideograms were used by various cultures in distant corners of the world.

Can you guess the meaning of these ideograms?

Although these picture-based systems addressed the need for more permanence in communicating, they were seldom helpful in transporting information over any sort of distance, located as they often were on the stone walls of caves or man-made structures. And for a long time, many cultures did not possess even this rudimentary form of writing. The only means available for transporting detailed information over long distances was by messenger. Messengers were relied upon to memorize information, travel—sometimes for many days—and be able to repeat the message accurately. Throughout the world, societies created special mnemonic devices, or memory helpers, to assist people in recalling spoken information. These devices took various forms. They might be sticks, notched carefully in response to the speaker's words—one notch for each important point. Or, they might be strings, sometimes of special colors, knotted in a certain way to represent numbers or ideas.

The quipu (pronounced KE-poo) was a knotted cord used by the Incas in Peru to keep records and accounts and to send messages. The colors of the strings, and the locations and types of knots, all had their own special meanings.

MNEMONICS

Did you ever hear of tying a string around your finger to help you remember something? It is an old-fashioned memory helper that some people still use today.

To help students remember the notes assigned to the lines on a music staff, music teachers use this sentence: <u>E</u>very <u>G</u>ood <u>B</u>oy <u>D</u>oes <u>F</u>ine. The first letter of each word in the sentence corresponds to the letter name of each note.

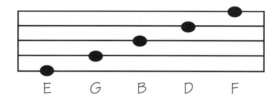

E   G   B   D   F

This same process can be used to help remember any list of items. Suppose you are going to the store to buy these five things: butter, milk, sugar, eggs, soap. Make up a sentence using the first letter of each item as the first letter in one of the words in the sentence. For example, "Bart makes soup every Sunday" will help you remember the list.

Over time, many societies became more and more organized and more and more elaborate. Advances in agriculture, architecture, travel, and trade brought change and growth. The desire for a permanent and transportable means of communication grew ever stronger. Merchants needed to keep records, heads of governments wanted to correspond with one another, and religious leaders needed to record beliefs and traditions. Out of these needs, a great deal of experimentation with a variety of systems began.

Certainly one of the earliest, and perhaps the first, efforts at creating a sophisticated system of writing began in Mesopotamia among a people known as the Sumerians. These were an inventive people who had already developed advanced methods of agriculture and commerce. They knew how to work metal and how to use wheels and sailboats, so it is not surprising that they were leaders in the development of writing. Of course, they did not practice writing as we know it today. For one thing, they had no paper or similar material on which to write. They had to use the materials at hand. Clay was dug up from the riverbanks and molded into flat tablets. Using a reed with a specially shaped tip, the Sumerians pressed wedge-shaped marks into the wet clay. The clay tablets containing this cuneiform (from Latin for "wedge-shaped") writing were then baked in ovens or out in the sun until they were dry and hard. This form of writing is so permanent that many of the tablets have lasted for thousands of years and can be read today by scholars who have unlocked the key to the meaning of cuneiform writing.

Each cuneiform symbol is made up of wedge-shaped marks.

The Egyptians probably borrowed the idea of writing from the Sumerians, since it is likely that the two cultures did experience some level of contact. The Egyptians, however, developed a completely different system. Their symbols, called hieroglyphs, were not at all the same as the cuneiform symbols of the Sumerians. Further, the Egyptians recorded them by very different means, painting or carving the symbols onto pottery or stone.

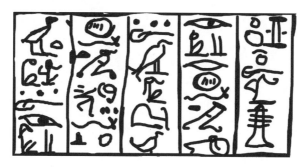

Hieroglyphic writing was used mostly to record inscriptions on stone temples or monuments.

The Egyptians made another huge advance independent of the Sumerians. They developed papyrus, the first form of paper, from the fibrous reeds of the banks of the Nile River. Papyrus had an obvious advantage over clay tablets: It was light and could be rolled into scrolls for transportation and storage.

By about 2000 B.C., systems of writing were beginning to spring up in cultures all around the world. In China, a very beautiful and complex system of writing evolved from pictograms. These delicate symbols were brushed in ink onto bamboo and silk. The Chinese language is still written in much the same way today. It is the only modern language that is based on pictograms.

	PICTOGRAPH	CHOU ERA	MODERN
Man	大	尺	人
Hill	𝆑𝆑	⚶	山
Tree	屮	米	木

Modern Chinese has evolved to include symbols that represent ideas and combinations of ideas. There are over 50,000 characters in the Chinese language!

If modern languages are not based on pictograms, then what are they based on? What happened to the pictogram system of writing? The problem with pictograms is that they cannot be extremely specific. They work fine for nouns like *bird* and *sun* that have obvious meanings, but more subtle ideas are very difficult to put into pictures. Often the reader must guess at the meaning. Gradually, most of the pictogram-based writing systems began to include some symbols that stood for the sounds of parts of words.

The Phoenicians of the ancient Middle East, a very successful and prominent people of their time, understood the need for a truly efficient and effective system of writing. They quickly saw the advantage of using sound symbols for written language so that every idea that could be spoken could also be reproduced in writing. Therefore, the Phoenicians identified each consonant sound in their language and assigned each sound an object to represent it. Usually this was a familiar object whose name began with the consonant sound in question. They created a simple written symbol to represent each object. They could have had no way of knowing that this seemingly small accomplishment would change the world.

But change it did, as the Phoenicians, on their frequent trading visits to Greece, introduced their simple but remarkable system of writing. The Greeks adopted the Phoenician alphabet, dropping a few symbols and adding several of their own. It was the Greeks who added symbols for the vowel sounds. This alphabet was shared with the Etruscans, the Romans, and most of the modern peoples of the world, whose alphabets descend from this very same system.

Today, as a result, we can record increasingly complex and sophisticated ideas for others to read and contemplate. We can save these ideas on the hard drives and floppy disks of our computers, or on the pages of our calendars and journals. We can send our thoughts in real time over E-mail or fax lines, or preserve them in the printed pages of books, magazines, and newspapers. For these abilities, we have many to thank: that first primitive man, who struggled to conceptualize the means with which to record a picture of a bison on the cave wall; the Sumerians who first used fistfuls of clay to form smooth tablets and impressed them with symbols; the ancient Egyptians, Chinese, and Phoenicians who found a way to improve upon the systems presented to them. Through their efforts and advances, they made possible the great wisdom literature of the world, and the creation of texts that hold the modern knowledge of mankind, a brimming cup of communication that we accept so lightly and with so little thought.

Writing is truly a gift from the ages.

Chapter 1

Scribbles and Squiggles

Get black on white.

—*Guy de Maupassant, French writer*

The spark of creative desire that lit the hearts of the ancient writers who worked with clay and papyrus still shines in the eyes of every modern child. Writing implements appeal even to very young children, and the urge to express oneself, which we see so clearly symbolized by the drawing on the cave wall, has not diminished over time. It is born anew in the heart of every human being. Though today's child may work with paper and crayons instead of clay tablets and reeds, the instinctual need to express remains remarkably unchanged. Just give a toddler a crayon and a sheet of paper, or place a preschooler in front of a blank easel with an assortment of paints and brushes. There's no doubting the meaning of the phrase "to make one's mark in the world." Writing is an adventure that says, "I'm here. I have something to say!" The forming of letters and the combining of words are tools and techniques that must be mastered so that the individual voice can be heard.

Because writing begins with the conception of an idea and the desire to share it, it is easy to see that the development of writing skills can begin at a very early age. A father talks, reads, sings, and tells stories to his infant daughter, knowing full well that she does not understand his words. But she does respond to his facial expressions and intonations, to the rhythms and the patterns in his speech, and as she grows, she begins to differentiate between the words and to understand their meanings. Soon, she is imitating what she has heard, creating sounds that become closer and closer approximations of words. Before her first birthday, she has a few simple words at her command. This is just the beginning. Her spoken vocabulary picks up steam. She adds words daily. Her comprehension vocabulary becomes enormous, enhanced by the fact that she has been exposed to a rich variety of conversation and a bright array of poetry and stories. The more she listens and speaks, the more she comprehends in an ever-widening spiral.

Obviously, the multiple components of language—comprehending, speaking, reading, and writing—are inseparable. A child's literacy and even intelligence may be profoundly affected by his or her first language environment. Children who spend their earliest years in a word-drenched atmosphere often show marked advances in school performance compared with those raised in homes where there is a dearth of conversation and reading. The learning of language begins at birth, or even before. It is never too soon to start sharing the joy of words, talking, reading, and singing to your baby. By doing so, you are setting the stage for your child's success in all the components of language learning. And, believe it or not, you are beginning the process of helping your child become a writer.

By the time she is three, a child usually has become a fountain of language. She tells stories, makes up songs, and delights in nonsense words, noises, and fanciful flights of imagination. During these preschool years, there are lots of wonderful activities that you can undertake with your child to encourage her delightful desire to express herself, to find her voice. Here are a few to get you started.

ACTIVITIES FOR PRESCHOOL CHILDREN

Retelling a Story

After reading a story, ask your child to tell the story back to you in his own words. Allow him to look at the book if he wishes, using the pictures as milestones to help in his retelling.

Dramatizing a Story

Use puppets to act out stories or parts of stories with your child. One simple way to make puppets is to draw (or trace) the characters in a picture book. Cut out the drawings and glue them to a tongue depressor or strip of cardboard. Or, use a flannel board and create characters from felt scraps. You might also involve the whole family by creating simple costumes and acting out the story.

Making a Recording

Label a blank tape with your child's name. Encourage her to tell a story, recite a poem, or sing a song. Date each entry on the tape for future reference. Kids love to hear how they sounded "when they were little." Also, this tape will become a wonderful audio documentation of her developing language abilities.

Taking Dictation

When your child has a story to tell, offer to write it down. A good launching point is a picture he has drawn or a photograph of a family activity. Ask him to tell a story to go with the picture. Have him sit next to you and watch as you write his words. Form the letters with care and use correct capitalization and punctuation. Display the finished product on the refrigerator or place it in an album or scrapbook. Share these stories with family members and friends, and periodically reread them with your child.

Free Exploration with Various Materials

Make sure that your child has an array of writing and drawing materials such as an assortment of papers, paints,
crayons, markers, safety scissors, glue, tape, and so forth.
Encourage her to create paintings, drawings, collages, signs,
and more. Give her old catalogs and magazines to cut pictures from. Save greeting cards and allow her to cut words
and pictures from those to use in her artistic creations. This
kind of activity helps to strengthen the small motor skills
necessary for writing. It also serves to encourage self-expression and to familiarize the child with a variety of tools.

Guided Exploration with Various Materials

Once your child has developed a backlog of experience
with paper, crayons, and pencils, he may be ready for some
guided play. There are a number of important concepts
that you can introduce and reinforce in this manner.
Some of the activities presented here include suggestions
for increasing the level of difficulty to make them appropriate for older children. Take care to keep a spirit of fun
in your explorations. Each task should be challenging for
your child, but not impossible. Your goal is motivation,
not frustration.

Pencil Pathways

To help your child gain comfort with holding and control-
ling a pencil, try this activity. On a sheet of paper, draw

two parallel horizontal lines from left to right. This is important, as the practice of writing from left to right is one of the concepts you are reinforcing here. To add interest, draw a little person or animal on the left and a destination for the character on the right. Don't worry about your artistic ability. Your child will enjoy your efforts. Or, you can ask your child to make the drawings.

Here's a sample drawing:

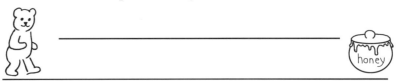

Ask your child to trace the bear's path to the honey without touching the outside lines. If your child has trouble staying within the lines, redraw the path wider until he gains skill. Suggest that he practice once or twice with his finger before trying it with the pencil. If he does it easily, create another path, but make this one more difficult:

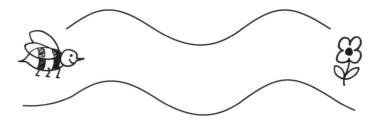

As he succeeds, continue to create increasingly complicated paths. Come back to this activity fairly often if your child needs practice.

A similar but more challenging task is to trace a single line. Using a yellow marker, draw a line from left to right. Again, include pictures if desired. Challenge your child to trace the line with his pencil, staying within the yellow mark. Begin with a fairly simple line, like this:

and move on to more complex lines:

When your child has mastered this task, he is probably ready to begin learning to form letters.

Identification and Creation of Shapes

Work with your child to make sure she recognizes and can name several basic shapes: circle, square, triangle, oval, and rectangle.

- Cut out several of each shape from colored construction paper. Ask your child to create a picture by pasting these shapes onto a sheet of paper. Talk about the shapes as she works.

- Use a yellow marker to draw several different shapes in differing sizes. Ask your child to trace each shape with a pencil.

- Give your child a sheet of paper and crayons in several different colors. Ask her to draw a blue circle, a green triangle, and a red square.

Directional and Positional Words

Work with your child to make sure he can demonstrate his understanding of basic directional and positional words, such as:

left	right
up	down
in	out
over	under
in front	behind

- Gather one or two little toys (such as a small plastic dinosaur or a tiny doll), a book, a block, a button, a shoe box, and a teacup. Place all of the objects on the table. Give your child one direction at a time to follow, such as "Put the dinosaur in the teacup," or "Put the doll behind the block." Then, let your child give you a direction to follow. If this is too easy, give two or more directions at a time!

- Give your child a sheet of paper and some markers. Ask him to follow the directions you give. Give one direction at a time, and at first keep it very simple: "Draw a red circle at the top of the page." Allow time to complete each direction before giving another one. Move on to: "Draw a green line from the left side of the page to the right side of the page." Then: "Draw three small squares in the middle of the page."

Visual Discrimination

These activities build your child's ability to replicate and complete shapes and patterns.

Fold a sheet of paper vertically to form a crease. Open the paper back up. On the left-hand side, draw a simple shape. Ask your child to reproduce your drawing exactly on the right-hand side of the page. Continue in this way, making each drawing more complex than the last by combining shapes and adding lines. Here are some examples.

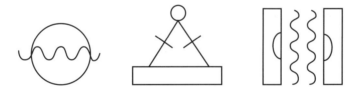

Draw a "squiggle" on a sheet of paper, like this:

Ask your child to add to the "squiggle" to make a picture.

Encourage your child to dictate a story about the picture to complete the activity.

Create a pattern for your child to continue. Begin with simple shapes:

Increase the complexity of the patterns.

Chapter 2

Letters
and Words

> If you would be a reader, read; if a writer, write.
> —*Epictetus, Greek philosopher*

Meg has just turned five and will start kindergarten soon. She loves to be read to, and she enjoys drawing and coloring, singing, and making up stories. She can hold a pencil and crayon comfortably and control the mark she makes with some accuracy, although she cannot consistently "stay within the lines." She has done many of the explorations and activities described in the previous chapter. She knows the names of some of the letters of the alphabet and understands that these letters represent sounds. She knows that a group of letters printed together on a page and set off by spaces represents a word, and though she cannot as yet decipher the word, she is eager to learn. Meg is ready for deeper exploration and instruction in the process of forming letters and words.

Some children get their fill of such instruction at school and need to spend their at-home hours in relaxation and physical play. But others yearn for more challenge and opportunity to practice and to learn. Unfortunately, the instruction in too many classrooms today is dull and mechanical instead of lively and encouraging. As a result, the child's natural inclination to express is stifled rather than stimulated.

Try some of the following explorations with your ready-to-read-and-write youngster. It's helpful to have an alphabet chart and chalkboard handy. Understand that your child does not need to recognize all of the letter shapes and know their corresponding sounds before she begins writing. As long as she understands the concept that letters represent sounds and that they can be combined to represent spoken words, she is ready to dive in— with your help, of course. You must stay close by to help her stay afloat until she gains sufficient skill and confidence, but don't keep her out of the water! This is the best possible way for her to get "in the swim" of writing!

For example, Meg's mother sits down to help Meg work on her journal. First, Meg draws a picture illustrating the subject she wants to write about. It is the family's trip to a local pumpkin patch. Meg draws her mom and dad and herself amid a vast array of orange balls. When she is finished, her mother asks her what she wants to say about the picture.

"Pumpkin patch," says Meg.

"OK. Let's write that. What sound do you hear first?"

Meg purses her lips and says, "Pumpkin patch, pumpkin. *Puh.*"

"Good," encourages her mother. "*Puh.* What letter makes that sound? Do you remember?"

Meg thinks. "*P?*" she questions.

"That's it. *P.*"

"I can't remember how *P* looks," frowns Meg.

"Like this." Meg's mother points to the letter on a nearby alphabet chart, and also writes the letter on chalkboard or white board. Meg watches and then writes the letter on her unlined journal page. (Directions for making a journal can be found later in this chapter.)

"What sound do you hear next?" asks Meg's mother.

"Pumpkin. Pum-*kin. Kuh,*" ventures Meg.

"OK. Do you know what letter makes that sound?"

"It's *K,*" says Meg. She is already writing a *K* on her journal page.

This process continues until Meg has recorded the letter sounds she can isolate in the words she wants to use: *pkn pj.* Then, Meg's mother writes the complete words on the page: *pumpkin patch.* She praises Meg for the letters she was able to discern for herself, and shows her where they occur in each word. She pronounces each word carefully, pointing out the additional letters and encouraging Meg to listen for these more subtle sounds. She explains that the letter J does sound quite a bit like the sound combination *tch* and asks Meg to listen and repeat both sounds so that she can make the distinction between the two. The entire process takes only a few minutes. Later Meg will show her journal page to her daddy and "read" what she and her mother have written there, reinforcing the many bits of information learned in the short lesson.

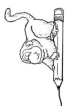

Invented Spelling

Some educators and parents are uncomfortable with this learning process because it involves invented spelling. By struggling with the letter sounds herself and working to make the proper connections, Meg will learn a great deal about letter patterns and spelling generalizations. It will take time and a great deal of trial and error, but it will pay off. The many critics of invented spelling represent it as "teaching" children to spell words incorrectly. Perhaps this is done somewhere in the world, but I have never seen, and of course would not support, such a practice. Children need to learn to spell correctly, but very young children must be given the freedom to explore without fear of being wrong. We surely don't expect one- and two-year-olds to speak perfectly. We encourage their efforts, though fraught with errors, and find their mistakes endearing. Just imagine how a child's speech would be squelched if he were limited only to the words he could pronounce perfectly! He could hardly make a peep. So it is with writing and spelling. The child's efforts need to be encouraged without limits. Otherwise, her writing becomes stilted and dull, confined to the few words she can confidently spell: "I see the cat." "I can run."

Beginning writers are capable of so much more. They have their own ideas and thoughts and stories to tell. I have taught first graders who wrote about mythic battles between Tyrannosaurus and Godzilla, magical pet bunnies, and the struggle to adjust to a new country. Had these children been limited to words they could spell with accuracy, their stories could never have been told. Once they gained confidence in themselves as writers, and learned that it was OK to use all of their words, they were unstoppable. Natalia (for whom English was a second language) wrote stories of up to thirty pages in length. Chaz, the dinosaur expert and old-monster-movie buff, wrote fiction that creatively juxtaposed giant creatures from the Mesozoic Era with gargantuans of the silver screen. Of course, before any of these stories were "published" and bound into books to take home, each child met with a teacher to revise and edit and correct spelling and other mechanical errors (for more about this process, see chapter 4), but it was through the use of invented spelling that these marvelous, revealing stories first found their way to paper.

Although it may seem insignificant, Meg has taken a huge step forward in her career as a writer. She is learning that she can create a thought and record it for her own review or to share with others. She is unlocking the secret of the alphabet and learning how to put its power to work.

The activities that follow are designed to help children who are at about Meg's stage of development explore the alphabet. Some involve writing—the actual forming of letters and recording of ideas—and others are simply phonetic games and exercises to help your child learn the shapes and sounds of the letters of the alphabet. Just do one or two activities each day, spending only a few minutes on each.

ACTIVITIES FOR KIDS
WHO ARE READY TO READ AND WRITE

Beginning Journals

Make a journal like Meg's for your child to use. Simply staple about twenty sheets of newsprint or manila paper into a construction-paper cover. Allow your child to decorate the cover as he desires using drawings or stickers. Encourage him to make an entry every day or so if he is interested. If he seems reluctant, create a similar journal for yourself and draw and write in it often. This is almost sure to win him over! If he feels that he "can't" write, encourage him to just draw a picture, and then allow him to dictate a caption or story to go along with it. After several sessions like this, urge him to try to write just one letter or one word before you begin to write from his dictation. With reassurance and patience, he will begin to write.

More Dictation

Dictation is still a very valuable tool at this stage. You can help your child with her journal, as described above. You can write letters, invitations, and shopping lists as well as continue to take down the stories that she tells. Encourage the telling of stories by providing some motivation. One way to do this is to create a "story box." Cover a shoe box with pictures of your child's choosing. These could be pictures of animals, outer space, and anything else that interests her. Inside the box, place a variety of small items that can be used to "build" a story. There could be small plastic animals and little dolls. There might be little toy furniture items, trees, fences, and so forth. Put in the box any object that might be used as a character or part of the setting of a story. Use the items in the box to act out familiar stories with your child or to make up new ones. Occasionally, record these stories in writing.

More Pattern Making

Move on to more complex patterns as your child is ready for them. One good way to do this is to make several rows of dots on a sheet of paper. Use the dots as a framework to create a pattern.

Ask your child to continue the pattern. As your child matures, she will be able to tackle more complex patterns. These are fun even for adults!

Homemade Books

Here are some ideas for creating books with your child.

- Make an ABC book by writing each letter of the alphabet, in capital and lower case form, on a separate sheet of paper. To illustrate your book, use drawings, stickers, or cut out pictures of objects whose names begin with each letter. Place the pages together in alphabetical order and staple them inside a construction-paper cover.

- Make a family book. Start with a magnetic-sheet photo album. Fill the album with pictures, placing only one or two pictures on each page. Encourage your child to describe the pictures as you record his words. Use colorful paper and stickers to add interest. Cut photos into fun shapes. Templates for this purpose are available at craft stores.

- Make an animal book. Find pictures of animals your child likes. Make photocopies or cut them out. Glue pictures of each animal on a separate sheet of paper. Record some simple facts about each animal on the page. Staple the pages into a construction-paper cover. Make books about anything that interests your child—a holiday she enjoys, her favorite foods, airplanes. The possibilities are endless.

Family Mail

Write notes frequently to family members. Place them in lunch bags, under pillows, or on the bathroom mirror. Encourage each member of the family to do the same. Provide an assortment of small pads, sticky notes, and envelopes to make this activity even more enticing.

Alphabet Activities

- Make a gel bag for practicing the formation of letters. Place 8 ounces of thick hair gel into a large (gallon-size) zipper-lock bag. Try to find gel that is brightly colored, or add a few drops of food coloring. Press all the air out of the bag and seal tightly. Place the bag flat on the table and smooth the gel into a uniform layer. Now, ask your child to "write" a letter in the gel with his finger. The bag prevents mess while providing a satisfying tactile experience. Rub the bag with your palm to "erase" between letters.

- Provide a similar experience by filling a shallow tray or pan with damp sand. Pat the surface smooth and then ask your child to write a letter with his finger. The enjoyment of "playing" with sand may make him more enthusiastic about practicing his letters!

- Use a yellow marker to write letters on unlined paper. (Or use paper with wide-spaced lines.) Make a series of the same letter, or write your child's name or any other word he would like to practice. Make sure to form the letters carefully and to leave plenty of space between them. Allow your child to trace the letters with a pencil.

Note: Be sure to use a yellow marker so that your child's pencil mark will be very visible, helping him to see the results of his own efforts.

PHONICS FUN

Letter Cutouts

Cut a large letter shape from construction paper or poster board.

Glue a number of small objects that begin with the letter onto the cutout. Buttons and beans might be glued on the letter *B*, feathers on the letter *F*, and a zipper on the letter *Z*. If you can't find actual objects, try stickers— ducks and dogs for the letter *D*, for example. Hang the letters in your child's room or the family room where they will serve as daily reminders of the relationship between the letter and its sound.

Consonant Collections

Work with your child to collect a number of small objects that begin with each consonant sound. As you find them, place them in zipper-lock baggies labeled with the letter that correlates to the sound. For *N* you might collect a nail, a noodle, and a nickel. The baggie marked *S* might contain a seed, a sock, and a small bar of soap. Continue to add to the collections over time. Now and then, ask your child to choose one of the collections. Work together to make up a poem, story, or tongue twister using the names of the objects.

Sound Search

Use old magazines and catalogs to hunt for pictures of objects whose names begin with a particular letter sound. Cut them out and paste them on a sheet of construction paper or poster board. Label the pictures and hang the finished product where your child can "read" it again and again. To add challenge, search for pictures of objects whose names end with a particular letter sound, or whose names begin with combinations of letters such as *st, pl, gr,* and so on.

Chapter 3

Sentences and Paragraphs

The difference between the right word and
the almost right word is the difference
between lightning and the lightning bug.
—Mark Twain, American writer

Kyle is almost seven and is nearing the end of first grade. He can form the letters the alphabet with reasonable skill. His letters occasionally float off the line when he writes on lined paper, and sometimes they are wobbly. Now and then, he will reverse a letter, writing *b* for *d*. He has some difficulty with proper spacing and will often omit the spaces between words. In short, Kyle's mechanical writing ability is perfectly normal for his age!

Kyle has not had any experience with invented spelling or journals. He usually copies material from the chalkboard and fills in the blanks on workbook pages or ditto sheets. He doesn't enjoy writing, and when he is given a homework assignment to make sentences with his spelling words, he rushes through it, writing the shortest sentences he can think of, using a very limited vocabulary: "I see a man."

Kyle's parents would like to see him take greater care and pleasure in the process of writing. They don't want him to be "turned off" by any facet of language, especially at this early age. So they decided to try to make the experience of writing sentences a bit more fun.

The next time Kyle has a spelling assignment, his father sits down with him. The first two words on the list are *like* and *bike*.

"What do you like most in the world, Kyle?" asks his dad. "What are your favorite things?"

"That spaghetti with meatballs you are cooking," answers Kyle, sniffing the garlicky aroma.

"What else?"

"I like the shark's tooth I found at the beach," Kyle replies after a moment's thought.

"Which one would you like to write about in your sentence?" asks Kyle's dad. He hands Kyle a sheet of scratch paper on which he has written Kyle's responses.

"Spaghetti," says Kyle.

He writes, "I <u>like</u> spaghetti and meatballs," copying the words he doesn't know how to spell from the scratch paper.

For the next word, *bike*, Kyle's dad engages him in a brief conversation about his bicycle, eliciting the information that the purple handlebar streamers are the most interesting feature of the bike.

Kyle writes, "My <u>bike</u> has purple handlebar streamers," again copying the unfamiliar words from the scratch paper where his dad has written them.

Kyle's dad keeps the discussion for each word short and praises Kyle for his interesting ideas and use of colorful words. His aim is not to lengthen the homework session, but to make it more challenging and more personal. Each time it gets easier, and Kyle gets more creative. Often, instead of simply writing down Kyle's suggestions, his dad will ask him to try and sound out the words before showing him the correct spelling, requiring him to think for himself about the letters and sounds that make up a particular word. At first this is hard for Kyle, because he is fearful of making mistakes. With time and practice, Kyle is able to do more sounding out and less copying.

Kyle gets good marks and praise from his teacher for his improved work. He has found that writing can be satisfying, and he actually looks forward to writing his spelling sentences!

Sentences

The sentence is the fundamental element of the written passage. Each sentence reflects a single, complete thought and takes a certain,

predictable form. The simplest sentence form consists of a statement made up of a subject and a predicate. The subject names the person, place, thing, or idea that the sentence is about. The predicate describes some action of the subject:

Subject	Predicate
The puppy	jumps.
Maria	laughed.
Time	flies.
The water	boiled.
A bird	chirps.

Or, the predicate makes a declaration about the subject:

The girl	was tired.
The photograph	is faded.
Teenagers	can be noisy.
The evening sky	is beautiful.
Truth	is important.

KINDS OF SENTENCES

There are four basic kinds of sentences.

Statement

> The boy scout troop meets on Saturdays.
>
> It is raining.

Question

> Do you want to go to the movies with us?
>
> Did Mrs. Merkin win the election?

Command

> Do your homework before you go out to play.
>
> Please paint the ceiling white.

Exclamation

> The building is on fire!
>
> Call the fire department!

Although we use the sentence to introduce the child to his first formal writing experience, it is important to refrain from making the mistake of pouring information about grammar and sentence structure into the ear of a five- or six-year-old! We don't attempt to impose the rules of grammar on the child's early efforts to speak; we know that he will internalize those rules as he listens, responds, and generally participates in the conversation of the home. The same holds true for the beginning writer. Although it is helpful for you, the parent, to bear in mind the rules and to use them as background for the activities you will undertake with your child, he must have the opportunity to explore and experiment. As your child matures through the writing process, you can use his own writing to point out repeating forms and patterns. In the context of his own writing, these rules and patterns will be much more meaningful than they would be in isolated examples.

The following suggestions will help you help your child to gain an understanding of how to frame interesting and functional sentences.

Sentence Frames

Make your child the subject of your initial sessions. On a chalkboard or strip of paper, write your child's name, followed by the words *likes the*:

Mallory likes the

Ask Mallory to supply a word to complete the sentence, such as *dog*. Write the word *dog* at the end of the sentence and add a period. Draw a picture of a dog after the sentence.

Repeat this process several times, each time asking Mallory to supply a new word. Go back and read the sentences together.

Next, ask Mallory to pick the sentence she likes best. Give her a strip of paper with the sentence written on it and ask her to write the sentence herself on another sheet of paper. Tell her not to bother with erasing, just to cross out a mistake and keep going. Remind her that this is practice, and that mistakes are to be expected. Some children develop great anxiety at the notion of putting something onto paper that is less than perfect. You want to encourage your child to do her best, but never lose sight of the fact that learning anything is a process and takes time, trial, and error. Do encourage her to keep trying until she achieves a copy that is reasonably neat and legible. If this takes more than two or three efforts, her small-motor coordination is probably not well enough developed to undertake this task. Go back to the activities suggested in the previous chapter.

If this is easily mastered, go on to more complex sentence frames. Here are several, in increasing order of difficulty.

_____ is yellow.
(Substitute any other color for yellow, or try another attribute such as hot, cold, soft, quiet.)

In the summer I will _____.
(Substitute any season for summer.)

The muddy dog likes to _____
            and _____.
(Substitute another adjective for *muddy* and any other animal for *dog*.)

Work together with your child to make up additional sentence frames.

Adding Adjectives

Once the young writer has written a few sentences and is comfortable with the process, encourage him to improve one of his sentences by adding an adjective or two. Ask him to write a simple sentence on a strip of paper. (Adding-machine or cash register tape works very well.) Suppose he writes this sentence:

I ate a pizza.

Challenge him to think of a word that describes the pizza. He may suggest *hot*. Ask him to find the place in the sentence where *hot* would fit in. Allow him to cut the sentence in two at that point. Write the word *hot* on a separate strip of paper and insert it into the sentence. Encourage him to come up with one more descriptive word. He might think of *messy*, *cheesy*, or *pepperoni*. Add that word to the sentence. If his interest holds, challenge him to find several more descriptive words, or make up new sentences to play with. Save the sentences in a large envelope and all the descriptive words in another. Use these to make a new game by laying the sentences out on the floor and finding the descriptive words that make sense in each sentence.

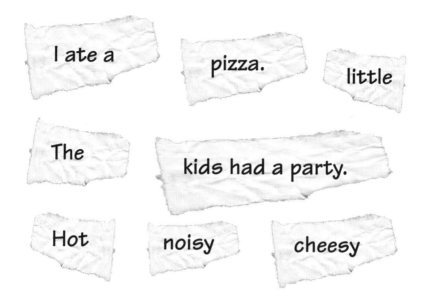

Word Banks

Word banks are collections of words that can prove very helpful to beginning writers. It is important that you involve your child in the creation of these collections so that she has a personal interest in them. Use poster board to create a number of word banks with your child. Print each word clearly and be sure not to crowd the words so that they are easy to read. Here are some ideas for word banks you might want to create.

Simple Words that are Used Often
 the, and, can, like, is . . .

Instead of Said
 whispered, shouted, begged, argued, complained . . .

Word banks are also useful when your child decides to write about a specific subject. For example, if she wants to write about horses, the two of you might brainstorm a word bank that looks like this:

whinny	mane	saddle	stallion
black	neigh	tail	bridle
mare	white	snort	hoof
reins	foal	bay	gallop
hay	pony	trot	oats

Combining Sentences . . .

Often beginning writers will use very short sentences.

I like football. I like kickball.

Explain that these can be combined into one sentence that reads more smoothly.

I like football and kickball.

. . . and Taking Them Apart

Conversely, some children's sentences never seem to take a breath. They are strung together with a series of *ands*.

I went to the store and I saw a giant buying some lemonade and I was scared and I ran home.

Ask your child to read the sentence to you, pausing each time a new idea is presented. Help him break his sentence into smaller, more digestible pieces.

I went to the store. I saw a giant buying some lemonade. I got scared and ran home.

Who, What, and Where

Cut three sheets of 9" x 12" manila paper in half lengthwise. Stack the six sheets on top of each other and staple them along one long edge.

Cut through the loose edge at four-inch intervals. *Stop about a half inch from the staples. Do not cut all the way through!*

You now have a flip book with three sections. On each page of the first section, begin a sentence with a description of a person or animal character:

A huge moose

A slimy snail

The grumpy pirate

On each page of the second section, describe an action:

> picked berries
>
> blew his nose
>
> fell asleep

And on each page of the third section describe a location:

> at the park
>
> in the fish pond
>
> at school

Draw pictures to illustrate each page. Flip open each section at random to create a silly sentence.

PARAGRAPHS

As Kyle progresses through the primary grades, he will grow as a writer. He will begin to put sentences together to express his more complex ideas. He will need to learn how to organize these ideas and combine them into cohesive paragraphs. For now, these will be simple, stand-alone paragraphs of two or three sentences. Your child in the primary grades will follow a similar process of building from sentences to paragraphs. Here are some activities to help him master the techniques needed to create well-structured paragraphs.

Define and Discuss the Paragraph

A paragraph is a group of sentences that work together to develop a single idea. It is set off from other text by an indentation of the first sentence. It generally will contain a topic sentence that states the idea to be presented in the paragraph. Each sentence should relate to that main idea, or topic. The sentences should be organized in a clear and sensible manner and should provide examples, facts, or details to support the main idea.

Sample Paragraph

Many people think summer is lots of fun. Children enjoy playing outdoors. The sunny, warm weather makes going to the pool or beach to swim a favorite activity. School is out, and families go on vacations or have picnics and barbecues with friends. Summer is a time of carefree pleasures.

Writing from a Model Paragraph

Using a descriptive paragraph as a pattern or model offers an excellent form of practice for your child. Short paragraphs that describe a character or setting are best for beginners.

Read the paragraph below with your child:

> Artie was a tiny and ancient little elf. He wore his tattered green cap pulled low so that no one could see his eyes. His beard was long and twisted into a point at the end. He bobbed up and down in a surprisingly merry fashion as he walked the forest paths, searching the woods for the leaves and roots that he used to make his magic potions.

Encourage her to write her own paragraph using this one as a model. Analyze the paragraph so that you can guide your child in patterning her own work after it.

- The first sentence introduces a character.

- The next two sentences describe how the character looks.

- The final sentence tells about the character's movements and actions.

Here is another example:

> The old house sat, tired and quiet, among the weeds. Its remaining panes of glass were clouded and streaked. Its roof was missing shingles and the porch sagged. A few stubborn patches of paint clung to the weathered walls, but it was

difficult to tell what color they might once have been. When the shutters creaked slightly in the wind, it sounded like the house was crying. This was the loneliest house in the world.

Again, analyze the paragraph to assist your child in using it as a model:

- The first sentence introduces the house.

- The next three sentences describe how the house looked.

- The next sentence describes a sound associated with the house.

- The final sentence tells how the writer feels about the house.

Look in the works of your child's favorite author for other paragraphs your child can use as models

Brainstorming

Perhaps your child wants to write a paragraph about dragons. On a large sheet of paper or poster board, help him brainstorm a list of words and phrases that relate to dragons:

scaly	guard treasure
imaginary	scary

eat villagers	long ago
huge	breathe fire
green eyes	swallow ships
big wings	live in caves
sharp teeth and claws	

Using these ideas as a guide, he can write a paragraph like this one:

> Dragons were imaginary animals from long ago. They were huge creatures with scales all over their bodies and great big wings. They had sharp teeth and claws and could breathe fire. Most of the time they lived in deep caves and would come out only to eat people from the village. Everyone was afraid of the dragons.

Paragraph Burger

This is a fun way to practice paragraph writing. Think of the top bun as the beginning, or topic sentence, of the paragraph and the bottom bun as the conclusion, or ending, of the paragraph. In between are all the things that make the burger, or the paragraph, delicious: details, facts, and examples. Remind your child to keep the burger in mind when writing a paragraph.

Chapter 4

The Writing Process

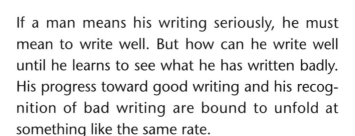

> If a man means his writing seriously, he must mean to write well. But how can he write well until he learns to see what he has written badly. His progress toward good writing and his recognition of bad writing are bound to unfold at something like the same rate.
>
> —*John Ciardi, American poet*

As your child gains facility in the writing of sentences and paragraphs, you will watch with amazement as these basic building blocks grow into a variety of more mature compositions. Stories, essays, book reports, and more will soon be within easy reach. It is essential for the budding writer to realize that successful writers—whether of poetry or of term papers—go through an important process in order to arrive at their finished products. This process can be applied to a business letter, a short story, or an essay for a college entrance application. Understanding how to use it helps a writer of any age to achieve his or her best work.

Though there are numerous ways to describe the process, in this chapter it has been broken down into seven steps. It is important to note that the steps are very flexible and should be viewed as helpful guidelines, not as rigid rules. Sometimes a writer will combine a couple of steps or eliminate a step. Other times, he may need to revisit one or more steps several times before he is satisfied with his product. Each writing task will require a different application of the process, and familiarity with the steps will make every writing task easier.

The writing process functions as a safety net for writers of any age. Every writer needs the motivation and "jump start" that can be found in steps one and two, the prewriting steps. These helpful steps bring the writer to the blank page with enthusiasm and energy for her subject. They serve to focus her attention and develop an eagerness that will propel her past the initial difficulty of getting started.

Once she is engaged in the actual writing (step three), she will feel safer if she knows that she is composing a draft and that she will have plenty of opportunity for review and revision (steps four and five). Ideas flow more freely when the fear of mistakes is minimized. Professional writers seldom feel the need to make their first drafts perfect, so why should young writers? Children feel more courageous, more willing to take chances, if they know they can make changes and improvements as they go along. Those familiar with the process know that they will have help in finding and correcting their errors and in refining their ideas. They gain confidence as they understand that their finished products will reflect their efforts and will be worthy of their pride.

Indeed, the last two steps involve creating an attractive presentation, complete with illustrations if appropriate. The young writer who learns to work with these steps can be sure at the outset that he will succeed and that he will be supported by the process itself. He will become increasingly able to recognize when he can skip a step and when he needs to repeat steps. As he matures, he will be less reliant on others to help him.

Beginners, however, will need nurturing and assistance with the process. Parents can help by becoming familiar with the steps and being available to facilitate each one. And don't forget to keep the child's age and maturity as a writer in mind as you work. Very young children need short sessions and only minor revisions for spelling, punctuation, and clarity. Older children can be challenged to consider complexities such as transitions between paragraphs, character and plot development, and matters of style such as mood and point of view. No matter where a piece of writing falls on the spectrum from simple to sophisticated, the process can help to polish and perfect it.

A computer with word-processing software can make the process easier. Even young children can learn to use this valuable tool. Chunks of text can be deleted, added, or moved around within the document, making revisions simpler. Further, the finished piece has a very clean and professional look. However, not every child has access to this technology, and amazingly, some teachers refuse to accept typed assignments. For these reasons, the process has been outlined here with paper and pencil in mind.

THE WRITING PROCESS

Step 1: Generating Ideas

Step 2: Organizing Ideas and Information

Step 3: Writing the Rough Draft

Step 4: Revising

Step 5: Editing

Step 6: Making the Finished Copy

Step 7: Creating Illustrations

Step One: Generating Ideas

The initial and often most difficult step in writing is to determine the subject matter. Sometimes the task itself will define the subject, as in the case of an assigned research topic or the writing of a cover letter for a résumé. Other tasks, however, are more open-ended. Your young writer may be asked to create a fairy tale or write a human interest story for the school paper.

There are several techniques that will help her choose a topic.

1. **Create an idea folder.** This can be made out of a simple manila folder. Encourage your child to collect interesting clippings from newspapers and magazines and store them in the folder. She should also place in the folder photographs and drawings that appeal to her. Encourage her to keep a note pad beside the bed to record thoughts that might occur in the drowsy evening or morning hours. Urge her to develop the habit of writing down any fragments of ideas that may pop into her head and may prove valuable for later writing—an incident at school, a brief description of an unusual or interesting person she meets, even a word or phrase that she just likes the sound of. Quotations, favorite poems, and even comic strips all have a place in this folder. Then, when the need or desire to write arises, the young writer will have a place to begin, an assortment of thought-provoking, personal resources to help her get started.

2. **Brainstorm.** This can be done alone, but it is much more effective if it includes at least one other person. Encourage all participants to be very free-wheeling. Suggestions that seem wild and crazy often move the conversation in a totally different direction, generating new thoughts and leading to terrific ideas. Friendly laughter is fine, but no put-downs

should be allowed in a brainstorming session. Make sure that someone takes notes so that good ideas aren't lost in the wave of energy that is sometimes unleashed.

3. **Draw or paint.** This method seems to be very helpful when a writer is feeling "stuck." It provides a shift in focus and can be very soothing, as it allows the mind to relax. Often the process of drawing or the drawing itself will suggest a topic. I have found this to be particularly effective with children in the primary grades but see no reason why it shouldn't work equally well with older children and adults.

4. **Do an "investigation."** Choose an object of interest to you and ask your child to do the same. Make a list of every attribute of that object. How does it look, smell, feel, and taste? What can it do? What sounds can it make? Be sure to include as many descriptive words as you can. Sometimes just the act of observing and writing will generate a new perspective or focus. Try going for a walk and finding objects in nature to "investigate" or use the same process to describe family members or fictional characters.

5. **Quick Writes.** These are just what the name implies, very short, quick episodes of writing. Choose familiar topics for quick writes, ones that

  b. shampoo

  c. face powder

 2. Nitroglycerin

 3. Livestock feed

Notice that the most important sections are labeled with Roman numerals and are not indented. Capital letters stand for the main ideas under each section and are indented. Numerals label supporting information or examples and are indented further. Even more specific information is marked with lower case letters, which are indented yet again.

When an outline is prepared in great detail, the writing of the paper itself becomes a breeze.

Step Three: Writing the Rough Draft

Before she begins, explain to your child that she will be writing a rough draft. Remind her that she should write freely and concentrate on what she wants to say. Give her plenty of paper—some inexpensive newsprint is fine—and tell her not to erase. If she wishes to change something as she goes along, ask her to make a single line through it, so that it can still be read. Urge her to "double space" her work by writing on every other line. All of these strategies reinforce the notion that the work is in a formative stage and that it is being written with revisions in mind. This may be difficult for children who are used to perfect-looking papers or those who just want to finish quickly. Many of them have been taught in classrooms that are product oriented rather than process oriented. Students are indoctrinated into this philosophy in the early primary grades. It may take a few tries before the new approach is comfortable, but as your child discovers the comfort and the improvement that this step brings to her writing, she is likely to embrace it.

Step Four: Revising

Though the draft may not be a thing of beauty to behold at that moment, remember that it is a work of art in progress. It should be treated with great respect, as should its creator. Writing is a scary business, and this step, which involves the sharing of a piece of work, must be handled with care and encouragement. You are going to help your child make improvements to her draft. This can and should be a positive experience.

Ask your child to read the draft aloud to you. Comment first on its good points: colorful word use, accurate punctuation, or a powerful topic sentence. Ask her to point out things she likes and doesn't like. She may have already identified problem areas such as a dull ending or confusion about how to use quotation marks correctly. It is important to encourage her to recognize her own strengths and weaknesses, so that she can become increasingly independent in using the writing process.

Discuss the concerns she identifies. Ask questions about areas that may need clarification or additional information. Focus first on issues of content and construction. Perhaps you will decide that a section needs to be expanded or trimmed, or that the ending needs more punch. One caution: Do not overwhelm the young writer. For the beginner, stick with the one or two most crucial improvements. Allow her time to grow into the process. With increased experience, she will gain comfort with the idea of revising her work. Your goal is to guide her toward her own discoveries and decisions. Her work should be hers, not yours. For example, if she has used a trite word, such as *pretty*, suggest that she consider a synonym. Show her how to use the thesaurus. Or, if a paragraph needs to be bolstered with details and examples, lead her in a discussion about the topic that will yield some suitable ideas.

When the two of you have thoroughly reviewed her work, she is ready to make written revisions. Encourage your young writer to use the blank spaces she has left between the lines of her first draft for minor revisions. Remind her to use extra paper when she needs to add longer sections or rewrite a substantial amount of material. Crowded scribbles are too hard to read and add frustration. Encourage her to give herself "elbow room" in her work.

Step Five: Editing

Revising and editing are closely interwoven steps. Sometimes they will take place simultaneously. Sometimes a writer will bounce back and forth between the two numerous times while fine-tuning his work. To simplify the process as much as possible, resist your urge to edit until the revisions to the content and construction seem complete. Then move on to the mechanics: spelling, punctuation, and grammar.

Use the chart on this page to help you edit your child's work. Of course, with the very young child you will work side by side on each correction, and the marks may be too abstract. As he matures, show him each mark and explain its meaning. Start with a few and gradually increase their use until your child is comfortable with them all.

Editing Marks and How to Use Them

⌣   close up space

∧   insert a letter, word, or phrase

ℓ   delete

≣   capitalize

/   use lower case

∿   letters or words transposed

insert space

?.?   hard to read or meaning unclear

Sample of Edited Work

The litt~~le~~ mouse slipped out ^of^ bed. ~~h~~e hoped

that the hungry gray ⁄at was asleep#as he

scampered quickly down the h ‿ all.

Step Six: Making the Finished Copy

When your young writer is pleased with her effort and that her work is complete, help her select the appropriate paper. This might be lined notebook paper for a school assignment, or a frilly sheet of stationery for a special letter. Make sure that she is refreshed and ready for the task before she begins. Urge her to take special care in forming her letters and observing the corrections made on the rough draft. (If there are oodles of corrections and changes on the rough draft, encourage her to make a second copy on draft paper before doing the finished copy. This will make the job of producing a finished copy much easier.) Remind her to take breaks as needed. The finished copy should represent her very best effort. Reward her hard work with lots of praise for a job well done.

Step Seven: Creating Illustrations

Many pieces of writing are more attractive and enjoyable when accompanied by illustrations. Suggest that your young writer enliven his book reports, stories, and even letters with artwork wherever appropriate. Discuss what sorts of pictures might be suitable for a particular piece of work. With your child, examine a variety of printed matter to see what kinds of illustrations are used. Encourage him to make notes and sketches on rough-draft paper. Provide an assortment of materials such as crayons, colored pencils, markers, and watercolors for him to choose from.

Make sure to demonstrate your pride in your child's work. Display his poems and stories in your home, and encourage him to share them with interested family members and friends. This will help him to develop confidence as a writer and inspire him to further efforts.

Chapter 5

Writing Poetry

A poem begins with a lump in the throat; a homesickness or a lovesickness. It is a reaching-out toward expression; an effort to find fulfillment. A complete poem is one where an emotion has found its thought and the thought has found words.

—*Robert Frost, American poet*

Children and poetry make natural companions. The rhythms and rhymes of poetry are as delightful as music, and as easily memorized. Quite young children know several nursery rhymes by heart and quickly learn hand-clapping chants, jump-rope rhymes, song lyrics, and commercial jingles. This familiarity with simple and accessible poetry forms a stepping stone on the path toward the enjoyment of richer, more complex poetic forms.

To help your child get moving along this path, make sure that she is exposed to a wide variety of poetry. Try to read at least one poem every day. Repeat favorites again and again, allowing their patterns to be enjoyed and absorbed. Purchase a couple of poetry collections for your home bookshelf, and check out others from the library. Investigate the works of a wide variety of poets. A list of recommended volumes can be found in the activities section of this chapter. Challenge your child—and yourself—to memorize a few cherished verses, both old and new.

Once she has been steeped in the richness and beauty of poetry, she will be ready to create some of her own. Try the following activities along with your child. Both of you are likely to be pleased with the results.

METER AND RHYME

Some poetry is written as free verse. This means that the poet does not have to follow any rhythmic pattern or rhyme scheme. Most poetry, however, is written in bound verse, which has a set rhythmic pattern and rhyme scheme.

The meter of a poem is really just its rhythm. This rhythm is determined by the number and type of rhythmic units, called feet, in each line of the poem. As you read the rhyme below, notice that each foot is made up of two syllables, with the accent on the second syllable. There are four feet in each line. Trying tapping your fingers or your foot as you read:

As I was going to St. Ives
I met a man with seven wives . . .

The feet in the next rhyme also have two syllables, but the accent is on the first syllable of each foot. Also, notice that there are only three feet in each line.

> I will buy some honey
> With a sack of money.

In the next rhyme, each foot has three syllables, with the accent on the third. How many feet are in each line?

> There's a place in my heart that I keep just for you
> For I know that your love will forever be true.

As you read poetry, notice which metrical patterns are most common and be on the lookout for those that are unusual.

The rhyme scheme of a poem is determined by the location of the rhyming words at the ends of the lines. It is easy to define rhyme schemes by labeling the first rhyming sound at the end of a line with the letter A, and the next rhyming sound in a verse with the letter B. Look at the various rhyme schemes presented below.

Twinkle, twinkle little star	A
How I wonder what you are	A
Up above the world so high	B
Like a diamond in the sky	B

Pease porridge hot	A
Pease porridge cold	B
Pease porridge in the pot	A
Nine days old.	B

Some rhyme schemes utilize more than two rhyming sounds.

Little Miss Muffet	A
Sat on a tuffet	A
Eating her curds and whey	B
Along came a spider	C
And sat down beside her	C
And frightened Miss Muffet away.	B

Sometimes there is only one rhyming sound in a verse. Only the second and fourth lines rhyme, but notice the internal rhymes in the third line.

Mary, Mary, quite contrary	
How does your garden grow?	A
With silver bells, and cockleshells	
And pretty maids all in a row.	A

Although there are a great many possible rhyme schemes, only a few are common. As you read poetry with your child, use the letter names for the rhymes to help define each rhyme scheme.

ACTIVITIES FOR BEGINNING POETS

Nutty Nursery Rhymes

One of the easiest ways to get your child started in writing poetry is by encouraging him to create additional lines or stanzas of a familiar poem or song. For young children, nursery rhymes provide the perfect vehicle for this activity. Look at the example below, using the nursery rhyme "Humpty Dumpty."

> Humpty Dumpty sat on the wall
> Humpty Dumpty had a great fall
> All the king's horses and all the king's men
> Couldn't put Humpty together again.

Notice that the first pair of lines end in words that rhyme with each other, and that the next pair of lines end with a second set of rhyming words (*AA BB*). Duplicate this rhyme scheme using different words.

Write out the first line, leaving the end blank.

> Humpty Dumpty sat on the _____

Ask your child to think of a word to fill in the blank. (Any one-syllable word will do. If he gives you a two- or three-syllable word, point out that the meter calls for a word of only one syllable. Most of the time, children will instinctively respond to the meter and choose an appropriate word.) Let's say he chooses the word *bed*.

Humpty Dumpty sat on the bed

Write the next line like this, leaving off the final phrase.

Humpty Dumpty _____

Ask your child, "What did Humpty do next? Remember, it needs to rhyme with *bed*."

"Humpty Dumpty stood on his head!" he might answer.

Write the third line, leaving out some key words:

All the king's _____ and all the king's _____

Challenge your child to fill in these blanks. He comes up with *kittens* and *cats*. Now the poem looks like this:

Humpty Dumpty sat on the bed
Humpty Dumpty stood on his head
All the king's kittens and all the king's cats

_____.

Work with your child to create a new last line. How might the kittens and cats have reacted to the sight of Humpty Dumpty standing on his head? Do you suppose they might laugh?

Humpty Dumpty sat on the bed
Humpty Dumpty stood on his head

All the king's kittens and all the king's cats
Laughed to see Humpty Dumpty like that!

Don't worry if the rhyme or meter is not perfect or if the whole verse fails to make much sense. The important thing is playing with the words and internalizing the patterns in the poetry. With practice, the process will get easier, but the results will likely be just as silly.

List Poem

Help your child create a list of characteristics for a person, animal, or object. Describe the things it does, how it looks, and so forth. Use this list as the basis for a poem. Here's a list poem about mice.

List	Poem
scurry	
sneak	Little gray mice
scamper	Scamper and run,
run	Scurry and sneak
nibble	As they search for food.
cheese	Nibble and chew,
crumbs	Cheese and crumbs.
chew	Stay away from that cat
search for food	And don't let your tail
big ears	Get caught in a trap!
long tail	
traps	

Place Poem

A place poem is a kind of list poem. List things seen, heard, and felt in particular place. What place does the following poem describe?

> Horses running,
> Ropes whirling,
> Dust swirling,
> Broncs bucking,
> Bulls kicking,
> Hats flying,
> People cheering.
> Somebody wins!

Concrete Poem

In a concrete poem, words are positioned to create a visual image of the subject of the poem. Here is an example of a concrete poem:

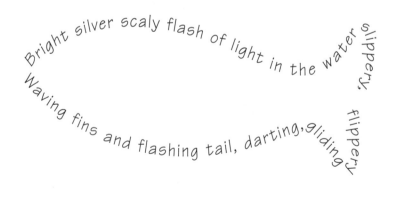

Cinquain

A cinquain is an easy-to-write five-line poem with a very definite form.

Line 1: Write the topic of your poem using one word.

Line 2: Give two words that describe or define the topic.

Line 3: Give three action words about the topic.

Line 4: Use four words to reveal one thought or feeling about the topic.

Line 5: Restate your topic in one word. This can be a synonym for Line 1.

> Daybreak
> Gentle, bright
> Glowing, warming, waking
> A time of grace
> Morning

Haiku

Haiku is a structured form of Japanese verse. It does not rhyme, and it usually draws its subject from nature. It is composed of three lines. The first line must contain five syllables, the second line must contain seven syllables, and the third line must contain five syllables.

> A pink bud opens
> Each shy petal unfurling
> First flower of spring

Acrostic Poem

Write the name of a subject vertically. Then give a descriptive word or phrase that begins with each letter of the subject.

> **C**luck, cluck!
> **H**ens come running.
> **I** have an apronful of
> **C**racked corn.
> **K**ind of you to give us
> **E**ggs
> **N**ice brown eggs for our
> **S**upper.

Tongue Twisters

Alliteration, the repetition of one letter sound, is frequently found in poetry. Tongue twisters increase alliteration awareness, and furthermore, they are fun. Challenge your child to tackle these tongue twisters and then create some of her own.

> Freaky Franky fries frogs.
>
> Six sleds slide on slick slime.

Rhyme Finder

Use this list to help your child find rhymes he may need to complete a rhyming poem. Simply go down the list, substituting each letter or letter combination for the beginning sound of the word he wishes to rhyme. Write down each actual word that you find. For instance, to find words that rhyme with sing, try each letter or combination on the chart with *"ing"*.

ding	sling	king
spring	ping	sting
ring	swing	wing
thing	bring	wring
cling	fling	

Save these lists of rhyming words for future reference.

a	i	qu	y	fl	sc	sn	th
b	j	r	z	fr	sch	sp	thr
c	k	s	bl	gh	scr	spl	tr
d	l	t	br	gl	sh	spr	tw
e	m	u	ch	gr	shr	squ	wh
f	n	v	cl	kn	sk	st	wr
g	o	w	cr	pl	sl	str	
h	p	x	dr	pr	sm	sw	

WORD CATEGORIES

Making a chart or table of words that belong in a particular category can be an enjoyable exercise to get the writer's mind working. Save each chart for future reference. They can be very helpful when the writer is looking for that "perfect" word.

Here is a sample. Other categories might include color words, feeling words, number words, and so on.

Motion words

run	jump	leap	somersault	fly
crawl	creep	tiptoe	slip	slide
glide	tramp	march	stomp	jiggle
wiggle	shuffle	dance	bound	soar
prowl	jerk	prance	bounce	toddle

SIMILES AND METAPHORS

Similes and metaphors are figures of speech that add color and life to poetry and prose. Both involve comparisons between objects or ideas. The difference between the two is that a simile is a direct comparison, utilizing the word *like* or *as*.

Her cheeks were like roses.

A good book is like a magic carpet.

The dancer's feet were as quick as hummingbird wings.

Cruel words are as sharp as knives.

A metaphor makes the comparison by substituting one object or idea for another.

The thick fog formed a blanket over the meadow.

The sunrise was a golden explosion on the horizon.

My baby brother has a button nose.

Tomorrow is an unwritten page.

Look at the list below with your child. Encourage her to make up a simile and a metaphor using each object or idea on the list. Try making up some of your own! Be on the lookout for examples of simile and metaphor in poems and stories you read with your child.

waterfall	peach	night	milk	kindness
anger	eyes	tree	mouse	snow

PERSONIFICATION

Another figure of speech that is useful to the young writer is personification. Personification is the bestowing of human traits upon objects or ideas.

The sunflowers nodded hello to the old man as he entered the garden.

An angry wind ripped Helen's umbrella out of her hand.

A thick stack of jolly, golden pancakes smiled up at the hungry boy.

Of course, the wind has no feelings of its own, and pancakes can't smile, but the use of personification adds interest and power to each statement. Work with your child to make up phrases or sentences that use personification to describe each of the following objects or ideas. Again, look for examples of personification when you read.

rain	luck	a stream	a hat	a pizza
sleep	morning	a fire	a diamond ring	

Suggested Reading

Here are some poetry favorites that you might want to look for in your local library or bookstore.

The Best Loved Poems of the American People
Edited by Hazel Felleman
Doubleday, 1936
Favorite Poems Old and New

Selected for boys and girls by Helen Ferris
Illustrated by Leonard Weisgard
Doubleday, 1957

Wonders and Surprises
Edited by Phyllis McGinley
J.B. Lippincott Co., 1968

Knock at a Star: A Child's Introduction to Poetry
by X. J. Kennedy and Dorothy M. Kennedy
Little, Brown & Co., 1982

A Child's Garden of Verses
Robert Louis Stevenson
Various Editions

Now We Are Six
A. A. Milne
Illustrated by Ernest H. Shephard
Dutton, 1927

I Am the Darker Brother:
An Anthology of Modern Poems by
    Black Americans
Edited by Arnold Adoff
Macmillan, 1970

Chapter 6

Writing Stories, Making Books

> A good writer is basically a story-teller, not a scholar or a redeemer of mankind.
>
> —*Isaac Bashevis Singer, Yiddish writer*

Children are natural storytellers. Even prereaders love to "read" the pictures in storybooks, describing the action they see as they turn each page. They are famous for the "whoppers" and "tall tales" with which they regale their parents. Often, they will sing made-up songs, crooning stories to their own rhythms and tunes. It's a fairly small leap from these activities to the actual writing of stories.

The advantages of written stories are obvious. They can be read over and over again for personal pleasure or for sharing. They can be saved and treasured throughout a lifetime. And they can mark the progress of the child as writer.

Watch for natural opportunities to encourage your child to capture a story on paper. If he is singing a story-song, offer to record it on a cassette. When he spins an elaborate tale to see how you will react, tell him it is such a great story that you'd like to have a copy. Ask him to repeat it as you write it down, then request an illustration or two to accompany it. Preschool children are usually full of ideas and imagination that bubble forth on a daily basis. All you need to do is take the time to catch and enjoy their merry output.

Older children, that is, those who have already spent some time in school, are likely to need more motivation. Many of them may already equate writing with work and have learned to be skeptical of their abilities. How can you help to rekindle their enthusiasm for self-expression? There are lots of ways, as a look at one family illustrates.

Eight-year-old Gordon likes to write stories at home. His parents, Ralph and Laurie, make sure that he has access to a wide variety of reading materials. They visit the library regularly, and each family member selects books to enjoy together and independently. Although Gordon is a fluent and accomplished reader, his parents read aloud to him every night, and they often enjoy reading aloud as a family activity. This provides Gordon with numerous models for good writing.

Gordon's family also creates many opportunities for him to explore the world. They like to do yard work together, and they talk about the plants and trees, the tools they use, and the weather as they work. They picnic in the woods in the fall and take canoe trips down the river in summer. Gordon has pets to care for. He participates in cooking family meals. His friends come over to build forts and engage in imaginative play. He is allowed to watch only a very limited amount of television. Gordon has an abundance of experiences that serve as background material for his stories.

In addition, Gordon has an appreciative audience not only for his stories, but also for his daily conversation. He knows he can count on his mom and dad to listen to him and help him if he needs assistance with his writing. They always show an interest in what he writes and urge him to share it if he wants to. His stories are carefully bound into covers saved on a special shelf in his bedroom so that they can be read and reread. Gordon's family is proud of his writing and they let him know it. With very good reason, he thinks of himself as a writer.

Recently, Gordon's parents have begun to engage him in some analysis of the stories and books they read together. They talk a little bit about the structure of the stories: the characters, plot, and setting. Often, they discuss a story's ending and explain their reasons for being particularly satisfied or dissatisfied with the author's conclusion. They may identify the theme of the story—perhaps friendship or courage—and comment on the author's style.

There is some danger of breaking the spell of a story by dissecting it too much, and this should be avoided. But it is possible to encourage young readers and writers to think a little bit more deeply about a piece by asking just one or two questions, or by throwing out an idea or opinion for discussion. Try it with your child. Listen respectfully to his response, and encourage him to support his answer with evidence or examples. It may be difficult for him at first, but if he finds that his thinking is accepted, he will grow more comfortable in his verbal expression, and this confidence often carries over into written expression.

In discussing and analyzing stories with your child, it may be helpful to review the basic elements of a story, which are described below. Remind your child to keep these elements in mind as she writes. With the youngest writers, focus on only one element at a time, for example, on setting or on character development. As she matures in her writing, she will begin to integrate all of these elements, but it will take time.

- The setting is the place and time in which the story exists, the backdrop against which it is told. Is the setting well described? Can you close your eyes and imagine the sights, sounds, and smells of the place where the story is happening?

- The characters are the actors in a story. Discuss them with your child. Are they believable? Is their dialogue lifelike? Do they arouse feeling in the reader?

- The plot is the action, or sequence of events, within the story. For small children, discuss plot in terms of what happens in the beginning, middle, and end. Older children can learn to identify the problem around which the action revolves in a story. They can also find the climax, which is the point at which the story reaches its highest level of impact.

- The theme is the underlying idea or message in the story. The theme might be friendship, courage, or the difficulty of dealing with loss.

- Style is the way the author tells the story. Style might be explained as the "attitude" of the story. It is serious or humorous? Does the language used give the story a dreamy quality or a gritty, realistic feel?

ACTIVITIES FOR WRITING STORIES

Here are a few activities you can use to help your child construct a story of her own when she is ready.

How-to Story

This is a good follow-up to some successful effort on the part of a child. Encouraging your child to explain "how to" do something will help her to focus on the sequence of events, an important aspect of the plot development she will need to use in later stories. Possible themes include:

How to build a sandcastle.

How to plant sunflowers.

How to make a pizza.

Sense the Setting

Often it is by the use of sensory words that a writer brings a reader right into the setting of a story. Work together with your child to create lists of sensory words. Begin your lists by placing each word on the list below in the proper sensory category. Do any of the words fit in more than one category? Write each list on a separate sheet of paper. Keep these lists in a file folder for ready reference. Continue to expand the lists over time, adding new words as they occur to you and your child.

Sound	Sight	Taste	Smell	Feel
sweet	soft	bang	green	
fresh	salty	hard	cold	
clear	bright	buttery	smoky	
jingle	reek			

Onomatopoeia

Onomatopoeia refers to words whose names are formed by imitating the sounds of actions or objects. Work with your child to make a list of these words. Here are a few to get you started.

crunch	click	screech
ding	whiz	quack

Five Senses Story

Practice using the lists generated in the previous activity. Use all five senses (sight, sound, touch, taste, smell) to write a description of an event such as a trip to the fair or a day at the beach. The event can be as simple as eating a popsicle or picking tomatoes from the garden.

Character Interview

As your child gains experience in story writing, he will want to know how to make his characters more believable. In order to do this, the writer must know his character well. Ask your child to conduct an "interview" with his character. Here are some questions to ask. Urge your child to add his own questions to the list.

What do you look like?

What kinds of clothes do you like to wear?

What do you do? (work, school, hobbies)

Where do you live?

Describe your family.

What three words best describe your personality?

What do you like/dislike about yourself?

Tall Tale

Frequently, young children will tell their parents long and inventive tales that they present as true. Instead of being concerned about these tales, let your child know that you appreciate her imagination. Encourage her to write her tall tale on a long strip of paper. Use a roll of cash register paper that can be rolled out to any length needed. Display the tall tales on the wall as they are told and see which one is the tallest.

Autobiography

Take out old photo albums and help your child select a series of pictures that tell the story of his life. Have a color copy of each picture printed on a separate sheet of paper. Then, take dictation or have your child write the story of his life (so far!) using the pictures as a guide. Encourage him to create one or more pages showing what he thinks will happen in the future. Staple the pages together inside a construction-paper cover.

A Good Thing/Bad Thing Story

This is a fun way to tell a story. The story must begin with some action or event that is positive. The next action or event must be negative, the next positive, and so on. These stories usually have a lot of action and humor.

What If . . . ? Story

During my son Wesley's school-age years, "What if . . . ?" was his favorite expression. "What if," he would ask, "the wind blew really hard and blew the roof off the house?"

"And what if," he would add before we could draw a breath to answer the first part, "it started to rain really hard and the house filled up with water? What would you do, Mom?"

No scientific explanation of the unlikelihood or impossibility of his scenario was acceptable. The "What if" had to be answered on its own merits and generally produced a fantastical story whose construction was cheerfully abetted by every family member within earshot. As the story wound down, Wes would inevitably attempt to resurrect it by adding yet another "What if" to the script. Here are some "What ifs" that may help originate some exciting stories at your house.

What if . . . an airplane flew over and dropped a huge sack of money in your backyard?

What if . . . a witch moved in next door?

What if . . . you woke up in the morning and your
teeth were bright purple?

What if . . . nine pirates came to your house for
breakfast?

What if . . . the water in a swimming pool turned to
Jell-O?

What if . . . you had a hippo for a pet?

Round-Robin Story

Group stories are always fun. Decide who will begin. Take
turns adding a little bit to the story. If you like, appoint
someone to write the story down as it is being told. If one
person tends to hog the story, limit each speaker to ten
words per turn, even if this means that the next speaker
has to pick up the story midsentence.

Bookbinding, Plain and Fancy

If you would like to make a more permanent binding for
your child's stories, try one of these methods of book-
binding.

A sturdy cover will preserve your story so that it can
be read and enjoyed for years to come. Take your time and
complete each step carefully.

Hint: Be sure to leave a one-inch margin on the left side
of each page of your story if you are going to use this
binding.

Materials Needed

- 2 sheets of light cardboard (9" x 12")
- The pages of your story (8 1/2" x 11")
- Large stapler
- Contact paper
- Scissors or paper cutter
- Masking tape
- Cloth or vinyl tape

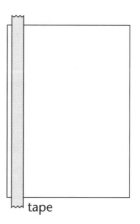

Cut a ½" strip, lengthwise, from each sheet of cardboard. Tape the strip back to the cardboard, leaving a tiny gap (about ¹/₁₆" of an inch), creating a hinge.

tape

Cut an 11" x 14" piece of contact paper. Peel off the backing. Place the paper sticky side up. Center one of the hinged cardboard covers on the contact paper. Press down. Fold in each corner and press.

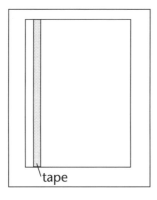

tape

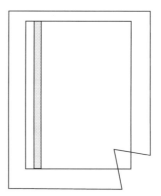

Now fold over the remaining flaps. Repeat with other cover. Cut two 8" x 11" rectangles out of contact paper and press one onto exposed cardboard on the inside of each cover.

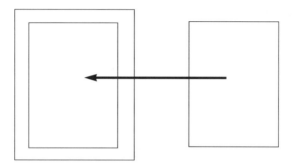

Arrange your story in the proper order. Place it between the covers. Make sure both hinges are lined up with the left-hand side of the story pages. Staple several times through the cardboard part of the hinge. Cut a 12" strip of cloth tape. Place it over the spine of the book to cover staples and reinforce hinge.

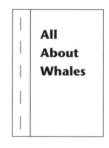

All
About
Whales

Shape Books

Suppose your child wants to write a book about butterflies. Cut as many sheets of paper as your child will need into the shape of a butterfly. Cut two butterfly shapes from construction paper for a cover and staple the pages inside. This simple process often adds lots of motivation and interest.

Accordion Books

An accordion book makes an unusual and interesting presentation. The directions given below result in a book that is 4" x 6", but an accordion book can be any size.

Materials needed:
18" x 24" sheets of construction paper
Scissors
Scotch tape
Light cardboard
Glue
Contact paper
Two 18" lengths of ribbon

Cut two pieces of light cardboard, each measuring 4" x 6". Set aside. Cut construction paper lengthwise into three strips, each about 6" wide. Fold each strip into 4" wide panels, like this:

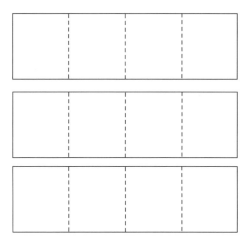

Decide how many pages are needed for the story. Tape the folded strips together to create one long accordion of the desired length. Beginning with the second panel, write one sentence or section of the story on each panel. The first panel will serve as the front endpaper. Leave an extra blank panel at the end for the back endpaper. Have your child add pictures to the story.

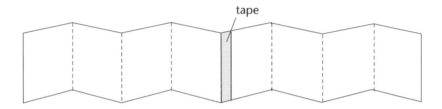

Cut a piece of contact paper that is 5" x 7". Place it on the table, sticky side up. Place one piece of light cardboard on the contact paper. Fold in each corner and press down.

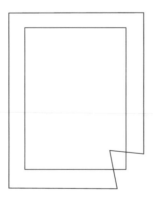

Fold over the remaining flaps of contact paper and press. Glue one ribbon across center of cardboard as shown. Repeat with the other piece of cardboard.

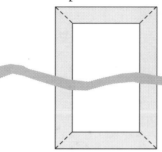

Glue the first panel of accordion story on top of the ribbon, leaving the ribbon extending from either side. Glue the last panel to the second piece of cardboard, again leaving the ribbon extending from both sides.

When the glue has dried thoroughly, fold the pages to close the book and tie the ribbons on either side to keep it closed. Decorate the front cover if desired.

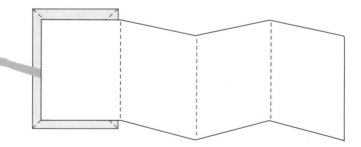

Chapter 7

Writing Reports

> I keep six honest serving men. (They taught me
> all I know); Their names are What and Why and
> When and How and Where and Who.
>
> *—Rudyard Kipling, British writer*

An important part of the elementary school curriculum focuses on the teaching of skills that relate to gathering and reporting information. Students are assigned simple reports so that they will become familiar with reference books such as encyclopedias, dictionaries, and atlases. Not only is it important for them to learn to locate information, they must also gain skill at digesting and interpreting what they read. Then, they must learn to organize the information and present it in written form.

Mastering these skills gives any student a decided advantage throughout his entire school career. There are a number of strategies that you as a parent can employ to help your child improve in his ability to locate information in a wide variety of sources and to package that information in a clear and interesting manner. It is also possible to have fun while doing it!

Begin by making sure that you do not limit research experiences to those that relate to school assignments. In the course of almost any given day, an opportunity for research will arise. Perhaps your child will ask you a question about some natural phenomenon that she has observed: Why do ants march in a line? What makes the leaves on the trees change colors in the fall?

Instead of giving her a quick answer, try saying, "Let's find out." Your interest in the information and your enthusiasm in the process of gathering it will be contagious. There is probably no greater gift you can give your child in terms of helping to develop her intellect than modeling the joy of learning for learning's sake. Show her that you are curious about the world, that you are eager to add to your store of personal knowledge, that there is much to be gained by this process irrespective of school or grades. Of course, your child's increased facility with research techniques will prove beneficial to her schoolwork, but this is really a bonus. Most importantly, it will show her the lifelong pleasures and satisfactions to be found in obtaining knowledge.

This type of spur-of-the-moment research is greatly facilitated by having a small reference library in your home. A good set of encyclopedias, a couple of dictionaries, a thesaurus, and a current world atlas comprise a basic reference shelf. Of course, Internet access is a wonderful research tool, as vast and ever-increasing amounts of information can be obtained via your home computer. But, as important as it is that your child be familiar with this incredible technology, she still needs to be able to use plain, old-fashioned books—at least for now! Place these books within easy reach. Watch for opportunities to use them, especially if this process is new to your family. Sometimes a television program can spark an interest. Find out more about the real-life characters from a historical drama. Read about UFO sightings after viewing a science fiction show. With practice, you will find that the active pursuit of information becomes easier and easier. You and your child will develop the habit of seeking to build upon the information that comes your way.

Naturally, this will involve some careful selection on your part. In this information age, we are bombarded with so much information daily—from television, radio, print media, and interaction with others—that we have to pick and choose. Think about your child's interests and your own. Focus on those areas that reflect your personalities, your hobbies, and your preferences.

When you make your next trip to the public library, look for a book or two about woodworking, gardening, cooking, or making investments—whatever interests you.

Encourage your child to do the same. This search may take you into parts of the library that were previously uncharted territory for you. When you get home, share the books you have selected. By putting some of this information to use, you demonstrate the practical aspects of research. It helps to show kids that books—and what's inside them—are of real, everyday value.

Once your child has made friends with reference books and the research process, gathering information for that school report should be fairly easy. However, she may need help in developing the methods she will need to tackle a more formal research project.

The steps in the writing process (see chapter 4) apply to the writing of a report and will be helpful, but there are also some important tips that relate specifically to report writing. Once a topic for a report has been selected, the next step is to gather information relating to the topic. Make sure that your child understands the meaning of the word *topic*. If this is her first report, explain that a report is a written presentation of her own understanding of the facts she will learn about her topic. The object is to gather information from several sources, and then to retell the information in her own words. Material copied from one or more sources is not a report, it is plagiarism. Explain that "copying" not only is wrong from a legal and moral standpoint, but it also defeats the purpose of practicing the important skills of combining and restating the information gleaned in the gathering process. The report must reflect her own work and her own understanding of the topic. The resulting product will be a true accomplishment and a source of pride.

Before beginning the process of information gathering, take a few minutes to discuss the topic. Encourage your child to make a list of questions she hopes to answer through her research. For instance, suppose the topic selected is penguins. Her list might look like this:

Questions

What do penguins eat?

Can penguins fly?

Where do penguins live?

Creating this list helps to focus your child's attention. It will help her to think about what she already knows and what she wants to find out, and will sharpen her curiosity.

Visit the library to check out resources for the report. Look over several books, but choose only two or three for the first few reports. As your child grows more familiar with the process, she will want to expand the number of sources she uses, but young children will likely be confused by too much information. Help her further simplify her research by using books or magazines from the juvenile stacks. Adult books are fine for background, and if your child's interest is strong you may want to check out one or more to read with her at a later time, but for the report itself, try to locate materials that are at or near her reading level.

Next, scan the resources you have chosen with your child. Look at chapter headings, photographs, and captions, and sample a bit of the text. You are not looking for specific information; rather, you are evaluating the books for their usefulness as sources. Choose the best and most appropriate books or magazines. This scanning process may stimulate additional questions about the topic. If so, have your child add them to her list. For example, she might add the question, What kinds of penguins are there? Perhaps you will want to help her reword a question. You can combine the first two—What do penguins eat? and Can penguins fly?—to create a more general question about penguin behavior: What do penguins do? This winnows the list down to three important questions, an appropriate and workable number.

Now it is time to take notes. This is a very important skill that your child will use countless times as she advances through school. You can show her several techniques for getting the job done. If she has never taken notes, don't be afraid to offer guidance. This is a difficult skill to learn, and your participation and modeling can be very helpful.

Explain to your child that notes are not taken in complete sentences. Notes use only a few words to convey a fact or an idea. Their primary purpose is to help you remember what you have read, and to provide a record of the facts and ideas discovered without copying someone else's words.

Show your child how you use notes in daily life. You don't use complete sentences to list errands. Instead, you use a word or two to stand in for the whole ideas. You might write "bank" in place of "Go to the bank," or "milk" to mean "Stop at the store for milk."

Here are other examples of ways we use notes.

Notes can be taken on note cards, but for a young child these can prove easy to lose. Regular sheets of lined paper work just fine. If you opt for note cards, use a large size. Encourage your child to write one of the questions from her list across the top of the card or sheet of paper. Another method is to use a sheet of poster board or butcher paper divided into boxes. Make sure there is one box for each question to be answered.

Now choose a book and read the pertinent information aloud. Pause after a small section of information and discuss whether it was important information for the report. If so, encourage your child to make a note of the information, placing it under the question to which it pertains. Continue in this fashion until you have gleaned all the information available from that source. Depending on your child's experience and ability level, ask her to do some of the reading and note taking independently. After a few reports, she will be able to do all of it on her own!

When you have finished one source, repeat this process with the other sources, allowing your child to continue using the same sheets of paper or cards. Remind her that she does not need to make a note of duplicate information. Check as you go along to be sure that she is recording each note under the appropriate heading.

WHAT DO PENGUINS DO?	WHERE DO PENGUINS LIVE?	WHAT KINDS OF PENGUINS ARE THERE?
eat fish	Antarctica	Emperor-largest 4 feet high
good swimmers	New Zealand	Adélie
lay eggs	Australia	17 kinds
like water	near cold ocean currents	smallest only 1 foot tall
can't fly	in colonies	all black and white
	in zoos	all have short feathers and webbed feet

When you believe that your child has recorded a sufficient number of notes under each question heading, stop taking notes. Ask her to choose the question she thinks would make the best beginning for her report. She decides that she would like to write about kinds of penguins first. Ask her to look at her notes, and in her own words, write a complete sentence based on each note under that heading to create one or more paragraphs. Discuss each section before she begins to write, and help her formulate a topic sentence for each paragraph.

Penguins live in colonies in parts of the world where there are very cold ocean currents. Penguins can be found in Antarctica, New Zealand, and Australia. They also live in zoos all over the world.

Penguins cannot fly, but they are very good swimmers and like to spend a lot of their time in the water. They eat fish and reproduce by laying eggs.

There are seventeen different kinds of penguins. They are all black and white birds with short feathers, flippers, and webbed feet. The largest penguin is the Emperor. This bird is about four feet tall. The smallest penguins are only about one foot tall.

Repeat this process with the other headings. Make sure that the report has an interesting beginning and a strong ending. See chapter 4 for the steps you will use to help your child revise, edit, and create a finished copy of the report. Allow her to add illustrations if they are appropriate. For a report, these illustrations may consist of drawings, cutout magazine pictures, or photocopies.

There are numerous styles of inexpensive report binders on sale at any school supply store. Keep a selection of these on hand to avoid having to rush out at the last minute to purchase one.

The Bibliography

A report or research paper should include a listing of the reference sources used by the writer. This listing is known as a bibliography. Here are formats for bibliography entries in the style approved by the Modern Language Association.

Sample Entries

For a book

Brown, Rudy. *All About Butterflies*. New York: The Silver Press, 1994.

For a magazine article

Glazer, Jennifer. "Toys That Teach." *Family* March 1992: 25–28.

For an article in the encyclopedia
If the article in the encyclopedia is signed, use this format:

Wittwer, S. H. "Parsley." *World Book Encyclopedia*. 1981.

If the article in the encyclopedia is unsigned, begin with the name of the article.

The Title Page

It is also desirable to provide a separate title page for most reports and research papers. Here is a sample:

The Mountain Gorillas

by
Daniel Palmer

Grade 5
Ms. Kelly Schulze
April 9, 1997

ACTIVITIES FOR FUN WITH RESEARCH

Use the activities that are described below to help stimulate your child's interest in research.

- **Play a game of Trivial Pursuit.** Allow players to use reference books to find answers.

- **Explore the Internet.** Your public library may have computers available for this purpose if you don't have one at home. When you are looking for information on a topic, you will need to type in key words for the browser to use as a guide for locating pertinent items. Try not to make your key words too broad, or you will be overwhelmed by the sheer number of choices the computer will make available to you. For example, if you are looking for information about hummingbirds, be specific; don't use "birds" as your key word. If you want to learn about training your horse, type in "horse training," not "horses."

Suggested Topics for Fun Research

Find out about the history of your pet's species and breed.

Find out about countries and cultures from which your ancestors originated.

Where does chocolate come from? Where does chewing gum come from?

Distinguishing Between Facts and Opinions

As your child begins to work, it may be necessary to remind her that a report should contain only factual information. It is not uncommon for younger children to have difficulty with this notion and want to include their own ideas and opinions in their reports. Use the examples below as the basis for a discussion on how to distinguish between facts and opinions. These are facts:

Penguins are birds.

Peanuts grow under the ground.

These are opinions:

Penguins are cute.

Peanut butter tastes good with jelly.

Sometimes, opinions can be restated as facts.

Many people think penguins are cute.

Peanut butter is often combined with jelly to make sandwiches.

Decide whether each statement below is a fact or an opinion.

Florida receives more rain than Arizona.

The beaches near Miami are very beautiful.

Oranges are good for you.

Oranges grow on trees.

Orange juice is the best breakfast drink.

Collecting shells is an enjoyable hobby.

Challenge your child to restate each opinion as a fact.

Chapter 8

Writing Essays

> What is written without effort is in general read without pleasure.
>
> —*Samuel Johnson, British writer*

The step from primary to middle school brings with it a new writing challenge. It is at this point that your son or daughter may first be asked to produce an essay. An essay is a short composition (a few paragraphs to a few pages in length) about a single subject.

Most essays are expository, meaning that their purpose is to explain something to the reader. Expository essays might tell readers why the discovery of bacterial life on Mars is important, clarify the meaning of a poem, or outline how to bake a cake.

Sometimes essays are persuasive. They make arguments that are designed to sway the reader's opinion on a subject. Persuasive essays address matters of opinion about which there is likely to be strong disagreement. Such an essay may argue the appropriateness of a school dress code, the question of whether the government should ban cigarette advertising, or the best use for funds raised by the senior class.

When the choice of topic is left to the student, it is important that the topic not be too broad. One way to help focus the topic is by writing a thesis sentence. This sentence should set forth one idea and give the reader a general understanding of the direction of the essay.

For example, suppose that Adam, a sixth grader, has been assigned to write a five-paragraph expository essay on an issue relating to the environment. He wants to write about endangered animals. But "endangered animals" is far too broad a topic. Even addressing all the issues pertinent to one particular animal might be too much for a five-paragraph paper. Adam needs to zero in on one specific aspect of this topic. After doing some reading and reflecting, he develops a thesis sentence that states the main idea of his composition:

The captive breeding program is helping to save the California condor from extinction.

Armed with this focused thesis sentence, which will give his writing a sense of purpose and direction, Adam is ready to move on to the organization, or structure, of his essay. The basic essay has an introduction, a body, and a conclusion.

The introduction should clearly set forth the composition's topic or premise and quickly capture the reader's interest. There are several ways to do this. Adam might open his essay with an image from his own experience of hiking with his family in Los Padres National Forest and watching a condor soar high overhead. Or, he might choose a quotation from a famous conservationist. He could begin with a short listing of birds that have become extinct in recent history, and explain that the condor could soon join this list. Other attention-getting openers include thought-provoking questions and surprising opinions. Often, the thesis sentence will find its way into the introductory paragraph.

The middle section, or body, of the essay provides details and examples to support the thesis. Each paragraph in the body presents a particular aspect of the thesis. The material in these paragraphs can be organized in several ways. Adam's essay about condors might be organized chronologically, tracing the captive breeding program from its beginning to the present. His friend, Pamela, who is writing about the importance of a wetland to wildlife preservation might organize her paper in terms of space. She could begin with a description of the center of the wetland—the water itself—and the many life forms it contains. Moving outward, she could discuss the vegetation that surrounds the water and the animals that make their homes nearby.

Other papers might be organized by presenting a general discussion first, followed by more specific information. A more dramatic organizational format is to present ideas in order of importance, building from least to most important.

The conclusion of the paper, the final paragraph, should "wrap it up" for the reader, giving him a final strong impression or idea. An image, anecdote, quotation, emotion, or action helps to create a strong finish. It is important to use fresh language or an original twist if the ending consists of a summary or restatement of the introduction.

Urge your child to use the writing process when developing an essay. Remind him that it will probably take several drafts and numerous revisions. Impress upon him that taking special care in the prewriting steps of choosing a topic and organizing his material will greatly ease the task of writing and improve quality.

Be aware, too, that many tests given in middle school and high school contain at least one essay question. These questions will be easier for the student who has practiced writing short essays. In addition, there are some specific strategies that can be employed to enhance his ability to answer such questions.

1. Read the question carefully several times. Underline key words.

2.   Put down your pencil! Don't write anything for at least a minute. Just think about the question, focusing on the key words.

3.   Write a mini-outline. Jot down the most important points or facts that need to be included. Number these in order of importance, or decide on some other means of organizing them.

4.   Write your essay, referring back to your outline after completing each thought or sentence.

5.   Proofread your essay and make the needed corrections.

To help your child enjoy practicing these skills, try the following activity. Choose a question from the list below, or create one of your own. Make sure that both you and your child know enough about the topic to answer the question, as each of you will write an answer in essay form. Set a timer to simulate test conditions. (Start with a generous period of time, say twenty or thirty minutes, and reduce it gradually as your child gains confidence.) When both of you have finished, read your answers aloud and discuss them.

> What are some of the most important things you can do to stay healthy?

What forms of transportation are used in your community?

Explain how to create a perfect picnic.

Why are trees important to people?

This kind of exercise demonstrates that writing is functional as well as creative. Being able to communicate clearly and factually in writing is a vital aspect of many jobs and a valuable skill. You may be surprised to find that your child's improvement—and your own—can be very satisfying.

Chapter 9

Writing Letters

> Letter-writing is the only device for combining solitude with good company.
>
> —*Lord Byron, British poet*

Letter writing is a great place to start helping your child learn to communicate. Letters that have come down to us through history reveal much about their writers. It may be instructive and enjoyable to share some of these letters with your child. Following are two letters by famous writers. The first is from Abraham Lincoln to his brother.

> Dec. 24, 1848
>
> Dear Johnston:
>
> Your request for eighty dollars, I do not think it best to comply with now. At the various times when I have helped you a little, you have said to me, "We can get along very well now," but in a very short time I find

you in the same difficulty again. Now this can only happen by some defect in your conduct. What that defect is, I think I know. You are not <u>lazy</u>, and still you are an <u>idler</u>. I doubt whether since I saw you, you have done a good whole day's work, in any one day. You do not very much dislike to work, and still you do not work much, merely because it does not seem to you that you could get much for it.

This habit of uselessly wasting time, is the whole difficulty; it is vastly important to you, and still more so to your children, that you should break this habit. It is more important to them, because they have longer to live, and can keep out of an idle habit before they are in it, easier than they can get out after they are in.

You are now in need of some ready money; and what I propose is, that you shall go to work, "tooth and nail," for somebody who will give you money for it.

Let father and your boys take charge of your things at home—prepare for a crop, and make the crop, and you go to work for the best wages, or in discharge of any debt you owe, that you can get. And to secure you a fair reward for your labor, I now promise you that for every dollar you will, between this and the first of May, get for your own labor either in money or in your own indebtedness, I will then give you one other dollar.

By this, if you hire yourself at ten dollars a month, from me you will get ten more, making twenty dollars a month for your work. In this, I do not mean you shall go off to St. Louis, or the lead mines, or the gold mines, in California, but I mean for you to go at it for the best wages you can get close to home—in Coles County.

Now if you will *do* this, you will soon be out of debt, and what is better, you will have a habit that will keep you from getting in debt again. But if I should now clear you out, next year you will be just as deep in as ever. You say you would almost give your place in Heaven for $70 or $80. Then you value your place in Heaven very cheaply, for I am sure you can with the offer I make you get the seventy or eighty dollars for four or five months' work. You say if I furnish you the money you will deed me the land, and if you don't pay the money back, you will deliver possession—

Nonsense! If you can't live <u>with</u> the land, how will you then live without it? You have always been kind to me, and I do not now mean to be unkind to you. On the contrary, if you will but follow my advice, you will find it worth more than eight times eighty dollars to you.

Affectionately
Your brother
A. Lincoln

This letter is from Benjamin Franklin to his British friend. Interestingly, this letter was never sent!

July 5, 1775

Mr. Strahan,

You are a Member of Parliament, and one of that Majority which has doomed my Country to Destruction.—You have begun to burn our Towns and murder our People.—Look upon your hands!—They are stained with the Blood of your Relations!—You and I were long Friends:—You are now my Enemy,—and

I am

Yours,

B. Franklin

Letter writing is certainly one of the most personally satisfying forms of writing. Not only does a letter give the writer an opportunity to express himself, but it usually brings him something tangible in return. A letter to a friend or relative can be full of news or self-reflection and can elicit a similar response. A letter to a company praising or criticizing a product will generally receive an answer. A letter to the editor of the local newspaper will often be published. If your child is a reluctant writer, these returns on his efforts can be highly motivational.

Additionally, letter writing remains a valuable skill. Although many messages are sent via fax and E-mail, they still must be composed using the medium of printed words.

The format for friendly letters is quite simple. A sample friendly letter is shown here. Notice the positioning of each portion of the letter.

June 1, 1997

Dear Karen,

I am really looking forward to my visit with you. Thank you so much for inviting me. All the activities you have planned for us sound wonderful, especially the horseback riding and overnight camping.

I have almost everything packed. I am bringing my sleeping bag, my camera, and my clothes. I made sure to put in a warm jacket since you said it might be cold in the mountains. Call me and let me know if there is anything else I should bring.

Say hello to your mom and dad and tell them that I can't wait to see them. We are going to have loads of fun!

Your friend,
Chelsea

When writing a business letter, the format is more formal and is designed to provide more information to the recipient.

---

851 Elk Court
Polaris, TX 78923
March 2, 1997

Ms. Elaine Docket, Principal
Roundmeadow School
228 Lupine Hills Road
West Fork, TX 78555

Dear Ms. Docket:

My family will be moving to West Fork over the coming summer. We will be spending a few days in the area next month and I am hoping to be able to visit your school as I will be enrolling there next fall. The best dates for me to visit would be either Monday, April 6, or Tuesday, April 7. Please let me know if one of those dates would be convenient for you.

Thank you for your time and attention. I look forward to meeting you and seeing my new school.

Sincerely,

Lynne Clark

A business letter should be typed, if possible, on good quality 8 ¹/₂ by 11" paper. No such restrictions apply to friendly letters. There is a wide variety of stationery available that is designed for children in fun and colorful shapes and sizes. Purchase a sampling for your child, or better yet, provide an array of papers along with markers, scissors, and colored pencils and allow him to create his own. Computers can be used to create personalized writing paper for your child, complete with his name and appropriate clip art. Many software programs can assist him in creating his own artwork, cards, and stationery. Make sure that he has lots of appealing choices for his letters and plenty of stamps. Purchasing attractive return address labels with his name on them, rubber stamps, stickers to seal the envelopes, and his own address book can all help to generate your child's interest in letter writing.

Look over the suggested activities that follow and choose a few that look like fun. Your child will soon be watching the mailbox to see what has arrived in response to his efforts. You will establish a habit that will bring him lifelong pleasure.

ACTIVITIES TO ENCOURAGE WRITING LETTERS

Create a Birthday Book

Of course, birthdays of friends and relatives present obvious opportunities for letter writing. To make this easy to do, create a birthday book for your child. Purchase a simple, two-pocket paper folder in the school supply section of your local store. Allow your child to decorate the outside. On the inside, above the pockets, list the names and birth dates (organized by month) of the people who are important in his life. Then, encourage him to create birthday cards for each person on the list. The cards are then stored in the pockets of the folder. Whenever a birthday is approaching, your child can simply write a note on the card he has made and put it in the mail. You might want to make a birthday book for yourself as well!

Get a Pen Pal

Exchanging letters can be a great way to make a new friend. To help your child find a pen pal, ask his teacher to put the class in contact with a class from a school in another city or state. A Girl Scout or Boy Scout leader could make contact with a distant troop. The magazine for girls, *New Moon*, has a monthly feature listing girls who are seeking pen pals. Ask the librarian at your local library for a recent issue.

Write Letters Requesting "Freebies"

There are several books that provide sources of free and nearly free items that children can get just for the asking. Here's one to get you started:

Freebies for Kids
by the Editors of Freebies Magazine
Lowell House Juvenile, 1996

Make a Pop-up Card

You will need:

    Heavy paper
    Crayons, colored pencils, or markers
    Scissors
    Glue

When a pop-up card is opened, a figure rises up out of the center of the card. These cards are simple to make.

1. Decide what the image inside will be. For this illustration, a bear will "pop up" at the recipient.

2. Fold a sheet of heavy paper.

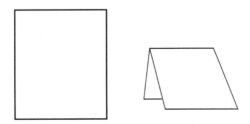

3. Unfold the paper and draw or color whatever background should be seen behind and around the bear.

4. On another sheet of paper, draw the bear. Color it and cut it out.

5. Decide where the bear should be placed on the card. At that location, cut two parallel slits, about 1/2" by inch apart and at least 2" inches long. The easiest way to do this is to close the card along the fold line and make the cuts through the fold. The longer the cuts, the farther the bear will extend from the card. (You can make more than one object "pop up." Cut a separate strip for each figure.)

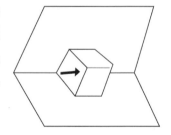

6. Fold the strip that results from the cuts back inside the card. (The original fold will be reversed for the strip and creases will be formed at either end of the cuts and at the center of the strip. When the card is opened, the strip will stand out from the card like a stair step.

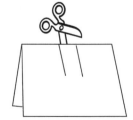

7. Glue the bear to the front of the strip.

8. Fold a new sheet of paper and glue the entire card inside it. Open the card. Complete any areas of the background that need touching up.

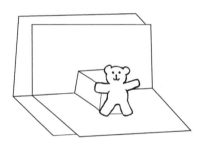

9. Write the desired message on the front and/or inside of the card.

Other Letter Writing Ideas

Write a letter to a company telling why you like or don't like their product or advertising.

Write a letter to the editor of your local newspaper about a current issue.

Many children's magazines print letters, pictures, and other contributions from their readers. Seeing his or her work in print is extremely satisfying and motivating for any child. Look for these and other magazines at your public library:

Cricket

Highlights

Stone Soup

Cobblestone

New Moon

National Geographic World

Check out one or more back issues. Read the magazines with your child to get a feeling for what kinds of children's contributions they publish. Find the address to which submissions should be sent. Encourage your child to submit letters, stories, or poems to several magazines.

Chapter 10

Writing Journals

> Writers write to influence their readers, their preachers, their auditors, but always, at bottom, to be more themselves.
>
> —*Aldous Huxley, British writer*

The word *journal* is derived from the French word *jour*, which means "day." A journal is a book to write in every day, to record daily happenings and thoughts. They present a terrific opportunity for all family members to get involved with writing. By creating a journal of your own and writing in it regularly, you are modeling a valuable behavior for your child to emulate.

The journal itself need be nothing more than a spiral-bound notebook. A scrapbook makes a very inviting journal because it has room for pictures and keepsakes as well as writing. A beautiful blank book from the local stationers may appeal to the romantic member of the family, and a diary with miniature lock and key might be just right for the secretive one. Just make sure that every family member has his or her own special and private place to write. Then, encourage writing. Bring out your own journal for a few minutes each day. Occasionally announce that you would like to share something that you've written. Make sure all family members respect each other's privacy, and that all sharing of journals is voluntary.

A special kind of journal is the dream journal. Encourage older children to keep a small notebook and pen at bedside. Suggest that they enter the date and a line or two about the main activities and emotions of the day, just before going to sleep. When they wake, before getting up, they should write down any dream they can recall. Place a flashlight nearby so they can record their dreams without turning on a light. Fragments of dreams and the feelings that accompany them should also be recorded.

Many psychologists, from Freud and Jung onward, recognize that dreams are powerful and significant. There is less agreement on the meaning and interpretation of dreams. Still, it seems apparent that dreams are messages from the parts of our mind that are not accessible to us in our waking hours. These messages can sometimes be used to gain insight into ourselves. They may help us tap hidden sources of creativity and imagination. You may wish to keep a dream journal for yourself.

Another way to bring journalizing into your home is to set up a family journal. This is an open journal in which each member records a daily message. Topics can be suggested by family members, or each person can write what he or she wishes. These can be fun and promote lots of conversation as well as the writing habit!

Below are some suggestions for journal topics. It may be helpful to try some of these as family discussion topics before introducing the journals. Since most of us are much more accustomed to talking than to writing, these conversations make a good starting point for expressing and clarifying thoughts and feelings before trying to capture them on the page.

On slips of paper, copy the ideas that follow. Place them in a shoe box or similar container. Allow family members to take turns drawing and announcing a topic of the day. Or, keep the book in a handy place and have a family member select a topic. Encourage everyone to extend the list by adding new topic ideas.

SUGGESTED JOURNAL TOPICS

Describe in detail what you see and feel at the beach.

What kind of store would you most like to own? Why?

Create a recipe for a magic potion and explain its magical powers.

Write about a person you admire. What qualities make you respect this person?

If your house was on fire and you had time to save only one object (not a person or pet), what would it be? Why?

What kind(s) of weather do you enjoy? What kind(s) of weather do you dislike?

Describe a friend whose company you enjoy very much. How does this person look and act? What makes him or her a pleasure to be with?

If you could meet one person who lived long ago, who would it be and why?

Pretend you have a month off from school or work and can take a trip anywhere in the world. Money is no object. Where would you go and what would you do there?

Are you a night person or a day person? During which part of the day do you have the most energy? Describe how you feel at different times of the day.

Do you like to be alone? Discuss the good and bad feelings that can come from being alone.

What do you do to help around the house? Do you think you should have more or less chores to do? Which chores do you like or dislike?

What behavior do you find most annoying in others? How about in yourself?

Did you ever give someone a gift that made them really happy? Write about that experience.

Think about the one thing you would most like to be good at. This could be a sport, playing a musical instrument, cooking, flying an airplane . . . anything at all. What would you choose and why?

Lots of things can be described as sweet—tastes, smells, even people! Reflect on what the word *sweet* means to you.

Why are birthdays important? Explain your thoughts on the subject.

Did you ever find something interesting? What was it? How do you think this item came to be in the place where you found it?

Chapter 11

Fun with Writing: Games and Activities

"When I use a word," Humpty Dumpty said in a rather scornful tone, "it means just what I choose it to mean—neither more nor less."

"The question is," said Alice, "whether you can make words mean so many different things."

"The question is," said Humpty Dumpty, "which is to be master—that's all."

—Lewis Carroll, British writer

Here is a potpourri of additional writing ideas for you to enjoy with your child. Remember that your participation provides important modeling and makes the experience more enjoyable for your youngster. Try these out and see for yourself that writing really can be fun.

Lots of Lists

Top Ten Lists

Making lists is a fun way to engage the brain in some quick thinking and a very nonthreatening way to get everyone involved in writing. Challenge each family member to make his or her own "top ten" lists of these topics and more:

Things that are fast	Things that are old
Things that are slow	Things that are new
Things that bug me	Good qualities in people
Things that are hot	Bad qualities in people
Things that are cold	Reasons to eat
Things that make	vegetables
loud noises	Summer activities
Things that are funny	Things that are orange
Things that are sad	Reasons why cats are
	better than dogs
	(or vice versa)

Word Lists

These lists are fun to brainstorm as a group. They are likely to generate lots of good-natured disagreement, but that is OK. The discussions will build your child's vocabulary and increase her awareness of words. A few sample words are included under each heading to help you get started. Save these lists. Later, challenge your child to make up a story or poem using several of the words on a list.

Words that sound like what they mean

slippery
mushy
melodious

Words that have a beautiful sound

Try not to consider word meanings as you make this list. Look for words whose names sound beautiful to you, regardless of what they mean.

amethyst
marmalade
lapel

Words that have an unpleasant sound

Again, the meanings of the words are unimportant. Concentrate on the sounds of the words.

gargle
cranny
flunk

Packing Lists

Pretend that you are going on a journey. This trip can take you anywhere in the galaxy at any time, past or future! Choose a journey or destination, and then challenge each participant to make a list of the things he or she would need to take along. Some possible journeys and destinations are described below.

> A mule trip into the Grand Canyon
>
> A six-month stay at space station Mir
>
> A visit to the Jurassic Age
>
> A backpacking trip in grizzly country
>
> A weekend at the home of George Washington in the year 1776

The Metaphor Game

A metaphor is a figure of speech that directly compares two objects or ideas without using the word *like* or *as*. Some examples:

> The fireflies were little sparks in the darkness.
>
> Her fear was a stone in the pit of her stomach.
>
> A river of wildflowers flowed across the meadow.

Write each of the words listed below on a separate slip of paper. Place the slips in a paper bag or box. Each participant will choose a slip and write a sentence using the word on the slip as part of a metaphor. When everyone is finished writing, read the sentences aloud. All slips are then returned to the bag and thoroughly mixed before the next round. If a player draws a word that has already been used, he must create a new metaphor with the word. Play for as long as interest permits. Praise inventive and unusual metaphors. At the end of the game, ask each player to write a new word on a slip of paper and add it to the bag so that you will have a fresh challenge the next time you play.

turtle	cold	eyes
hunger	bear	bee
moon	anger	love
fire	ocean	clouds
blanket	heat	hair

Left Out Letters

Write each letter of the alphabet on a separate slip of paper. Put the slips in a box or a paper bag. Mix them up, then draw one letter. Work with your child to write a sentence, paragraph, or brief story (depending on your child's ability level) without using the "left out letter." Or, each of you might draw a letter and work independently to create sentences or stories. If you really want a challenge, try leaving out two or more letters at a time!

Expandable Sentences

This game will give you and your child practice in using descriptive language. Starting with one short sentence, each participant takes a turn adding a descriptive word. Here is a sample:

> The fish swam in the water.
>
> The tiny fish swam in the water.
>
> The tiny, silver fish swam in the water.
>
> The tiny, silver fish swam in the cool water.
>
> The tiny, silver fish swam in the cool, blue water.
>
> The tiny, silver fish swam lazily in the cool, blue water.

Write one of the sentences below on a large sheet of paper so that all participants can see it. Continue adding to the sentence until the group decides that it has been sufficiently expanded. Then, go on to another sentence. When you run out of sentences, create your own!

The giant slept in his bed.

A man looked at his car.

The boy ate the ice cream.

The band played a song.

A mouse crept out into the night.

Finish the Story

This game is best when three or more people are playing. Each player needs a sheet of paper and a pencil. Each person writes an incomplete sentence at the top of his sheet of paper. Papers are then passed to the left. The next player finishes the sentence and folds down the top of the paper. Then, he begins another sentence and again passes the paper to the left. With each round, players complete a sentence, fold the paper down, and begin a new sentence before passing the paper on. After an agreed-upon number of rounds (five or six is a good number), players complete the sentence and do not add a new beginning. At this point, all papers are unfolded and read aloud.

Here's an example:

Johnny got up one morning and
(Pass to player on left.)

Johnny got up one morning and <u>ate breakfast</u>.

(Paper is folded so that next player cannot see this sentence.)

He ate a huge
(Pass to player on left.)

He ate a huge <u>watermelon and spit out all the seeds</u>.
(Paper is folded so that the next player cannot see this sentence.)

They splattered all over
(Pass to player on left. Play continues in this manner.)

Trading Places

Just for fun, trade perspectives with your child. You will write a description of your child's "typical" day from her point of view. She will write a description of your "typical" day from your point of view. Each of you should try to use the vocabulary and attitude of the other. When you have finished writing, read and discuss each piece and be prepared for some interesting insights!

Remember that you can go back to the games and activities in this and other chapters time and time again. Add your own twists and extensions to each exploration. With experience will come an abundance of new ideas and the understanding that writing is not only a tool to be utilized but an adventure to be savored. Write on!

Other books that will help develop your child's gifts and talents:

How to Develop Your Child's Gifts and Talents through the Elementary Years—Grades 1-5
$11.95/6 x 9/144 pp/paper/ISBN 1-56565-165-0

How to Develop Your Child's Gifts and Talents in Math
$15.00/6 x 9/176 pp/paper/ISBN 1-56565-338-6

How to Develop Your Child's Gifts and Talents in Reading
$15.00/6 x 9/224 pp/paper/ISBN 1-56565-447-1

How to Develop Your Child's Gifts and Talents in Vocabulary
$15.00/6 x 9/192 pp/paper/ISBN 1-56565-637-7

Thinking Games to Play with Your Child
$13.00/6 x 9/176 pp/paper/ISBN 1-56565-810-8

101 Amusing Ways to Develop Your Child's Thinking Skills & Creativity
$13.00/6 x 9/208 pp/paper/ISBN 1-56565-479-X

Teach Your Child Math
$15.00/6 x 9/208 pp/paper/ISBN 1-56565-481-1

Teach Your Child Science
$12.95/6 x 9/192 pp/paper/ISBN 1-56565-347-5

Teach Your Child to Draw
$15.00/7 1/2 x 9 1/4/160 pp/paper/0-929923-25-1

Available at your local bookstore or
Send a check or money order, plus shipping charges to:

Department PL
Lowell House
2020 Avenue of the Stars, Suite 300
Los Angeles, CA 90067

For special or bulk sales, call (310) 552-7555, ext. 30